Botham
REKINDLES THE
Ashes

Front cover photograph by Adrian Murrell, All-Sport.

The last innings at Edgbaston. A wicket England badly needed. Emburey has Yallop caught off bat and pad by Botham and Australia begin their slide from 87 for three to 121 all out.

Botham REKINDLES THE Ashes

The Daily Telegraph story of the '81 Test Series

Michael Melford

𝕮𝖍𝖊 𝕯𝖆𝖎𝖑𝖞 𝕿𝖊𝖑𝖊𝖌𝖗𝖆𝖕𝖍

Published by The Daily Telegraph
135 Fleet Street, London EC4P 4BL

First Published 1981
© Daily Telegraph 1981
Scorecharts © Bill Frindall 1981
ISBN 0 901684 68 6 paperback
ISBN 0 901684 69 4 hardback

Design by Martin Bronkhorst

All photographs except Old bowling Border and
Willis yorking Bright by Adrian Murrell,
All-Sport.

Printed in Great Britain by
Biddles Ltd, Guildford, Surrey

Contents

Foreword by Peter May, President of M.C.C.   vi

**Introduction by Michael Melford, cricket correspondent
for The Daily Telegraph**   1

**An Australian View by Peter McFarline, chief cricket writer
for The Age, Melbourne**   5

**Day by Day reports from The Daily Telegraph
by Michael Melford**

The First Test, Trent Bridge   9
The Second Test, Lords   23
The Third Test, Headingley   43
Sydney, 1894 – The Only Parallel by E. W. Swanton,
    former cricket correspondent for The Daily Telegraph   64
The Fourth Test, Edgbaston   65
The Fifth Test, Old Trafford   81
The Sixth Test, The Oval   101

The Series in Figures by Bill Frindall

The First Test   124
The Second Test   128
The Third Test   132
The Fourth Test   136
The Fifth Test   140
The Sixth Test   144
Test Match Summary   148
Test Career Records – England   152
Test Career Records – Australia   153
Ian Botham's 149 at Headingly   154
Ian Botham's 118 at Old Trafford   155

Epilogue by E. W. Swanton   **156**

Foreword

As an avid reader of *The Daily Telegraph* reports, I am delighted to know that this book has been put together.

There is no doubt that this series has revitalised interest in Test cricket, and the dramatic results from Headingley, Edgbaston and Old Trafford have been received with acclaim everywhere. So many people have been genuinely delighted at the success of England and the remarkable all round performances of Ian Botham. I personally will never forget those magnificent strokes which ended up in the back of the stand.

I am sure you will enjoy reviving these memories.

Lord's   *Peter May*
September 1981   *President of M.C.C.*

Introduction

It was the abruptness and improbability of the transition, not only the spectacular way in which it was achieved, which captured the public imagination in the Cornhill Test series 1981 and still makes those who watched it wonder if it really happened.

At three o'clock on Monday July 20 England, who had followed on 227 behind, were still 92 runs short of saving an innings defeat and had only three wickets left. In the first innings the last three wickets had mustered only 19 runs. Plans were well advanced on all sides for an imminent return home with England 2-0 down in the series. Exactly four weeks later they had won the series 3-1.

There were other contrasts too. The first part of the 1981 season had been no advertisement for the game. May had been wet, June cold and the cricket correspondingly unattractive. Yet from early July the summer redeemed itself, reaching new heights of magnanimity during the Edgbaston Test when the weather was fresh and sunny in Birmingham while it rained persistently in London.

The fortunes of individual players underwent similar staggering changes. In 12 matches under his own captaincy Ian Botham had been barely recognisable as the gifted all-rounder who had reached 1,000 runs and 100 wickets in Test cricket in fewer matches than any other player. In the most recent Test at Lord's he had made a 'pair'.

With Botham's resignation on the last day at Lord's, coinciding with the selectors' decision to restore Mike Brearley as captain, there came the marvellous return to former glories – the match-winning 149 not out of Headingley, the five wickets for one run at Edgbaston, the 114 at Old Trafford which is generally accepted as one of the best Test innings of its type ever played. When not fully fit, he still took 10 wickets in the Sixth Test. Even his catching recovered its former brilliance.

Bob Willis was another whose fortunes changed in an extraordinary way at Headingley. His nought for 72 in the first innings must have made many, including the selectors, think that at 32 his long and honourable Test career was over. Yet his eight for 43 in the second innings when Australia needed only 130 to win will go down as one of the most momentous pieces of bowling in Test history.

1

It was not widely known at the time that through a misunderstanding Willis was not in the team which the selectors originally chose for Headingley. They were mistakenly informed that his absence from the Warwickshire side that week-end was because he had not recovered from a chest infection suffered in the previous Test. In fact, it was to make absolutely sure that he would be fit for Headingley and he was restored to the Test team before it was announced.

I thought after the Prudential series in early June and with still more conviction after the first two-and-a-half Tests that Australia would win the series. They would not necessarily bat better but would bowl better on the good batting pitches to be expected later in the summer.

Limited-over cricket is not ordinarily a reliable guide – in Australia in 1979-80 England won all four one-day matches against Australia and lost all three Test matches – but in this Prudential series there were signs that a youngish Australian side would improve during the season.

They had had a wretched start in the rains of May and England began the Prudential series having won all their last six limited-over matches against them. The first match at Lord's went much as expected, though even in that there were indications that the younger Australian bowlers, Lawson and Alderman, were going to prove highly effective in England.

Two days later this was confirmed when Australia won by two runs at Edgbaston and two days after that they won easily at Headingley, bowling much too well for England.

When, unlike England, they held their catches at Trent Bridge on the sort of pitch on which England usually have an advantage, when they displayed the bulk of the virtues at Lord's and on the first $3\frac{1}{2}$ days at Headingley, the trend of events seemed to be entirely predictable. One was not to know then that Lawson would not play again on the tour and that good batting pitches would be in short supply until the final Test at the Oval.

Many of the events which followed had not happened for around 100 years and will not happen again in a hurry.

Prompted by many letters, I wrote of the similarity of the Headingley Test to "Fowler's Match" – Eton and Harrow at Lord's in 1910. Eton, having followed on, led by only four runs with nine second innings wickets gone but eventually bowled out Harrow for 45 to win by nine runs.

Many more readers wrote then with memories of that distant

day and of a finish involving the future Field Marshal Earl Alexander of Tunis. (One wrote, with feeling, of the fiery pace of Guy Earle, the Harrow captain, at his prep school when Sandroyd routed Cheam in 1904.) No great imagination was needed to foresee the 1981 Test series and especially the Headingley Test becoming just as colourful a part of cricket history as "Fowler's Match."

People remember "Fowler's Match" as a magnificent cricket match even though they may have had Harrow sympathies or no affinity with either side.

Obviously in 1981 it has been highly gratifying for the English cricket public, that huge, opinionated and unidentifiable body stretching far beyond the gates of cricket grounds into some unlikely places, to taste success again after a barren spell.

But cricket of the fluctuating character played this summer is not just the property of one side. I have no doubt that when the disappointment has faded or been superseded by success, cricketers in Australia and indeed in countries not involved, will come to marvel at the things which happened in 1981 – just as cricketers far away from Australia still marvel at what Sir Donald Bradman did in the 1930s.

Michael Melford

An Australian View

The image of Australians as sun worshippers has taken a nasty beating. For when the sun finally shone on the 1981 tourists, they went from Ashes winners to series losers in the space of six weeks. The dank and dark days of June and early July, the Australians handled with aplomb. They collected the Prudential Trophy over three one-day games for the first time, won the first Test at Nottingham by four wickets and had little difficulty in drawing the second encounter at Lord's.

Then came Leeds and our first taste of what was a belated summer. Instead of the Australians, it was Ian Botham, Bob Willis and Mike Brearley who basked in a collection of incredible reversals that rejuvenated popular interest in the game here, proved an unheralded financial bonanza for the Test and County Cricket Board and did a fair job of the impossible – keeping football away from the sporting headlines well into September.

That was scant reward for the tourists, many of whom performed well above expectation. But it also served to underline a widespread batting weakness that had shown itself occasionally in Australia in the past few years. Early in February 1981, the Australian side was bowled out on the last day of the Third Test against India for 84 runs on an unpredictable Melbourne Cricket Ground wicket. That team included Greg Chappell.

The team that was bowled out at Leeds for 111 (second innings), 121 at Birmingham (second innings) and 130 (Manchester first innings) did not have Greg Chappell, who was unavailable for the tour for family and business reasons. Neither did it have a high-class batsman who was able, under pressure, to withstand the assault of the England pace bowlers and provide the inspiration for other members of the squad. Therein lies the major disappointment of the tour. Kim Hughes, hero of the 1980 Centenary Test at Lord's with innings of 117 and 84, proved capable in almost every respect of his new job as captain of Australia. But Hughes suffered technical rather than mental difficulties with his batting, scoring only 300 runs in 12 innings at an average of 25.00 – rather below his normal Test contribution of 42.37 an innings. Seven times he fell an lbw victim to the England bowlers, who were able to bring the ball back late on him, taking advantage of his hard-wicket habit of playing across the line of flight.

Although figures will show that the left-handed Allan Border was the most successful batsman on either side – 533 runs at 59.22 – it should be pointed out that in the games Australia lost (the Third, Fourth and Fifth Tests) he scored only 8,0,2,40,11 and 123 not out. By the time he reached the peak of his form with 123 not out at Manchester, Australia had been set 506 runs to win. No team in the history of Test cricket has come within 100 runs of such an achievement.

The series, then, was decided as much on the inability of the Australian batsmen to master the requirements of batting on English wickets as it was on the breath-taking all-round skills of Botham and the furious, sometimes inspired fast bowling of Willis and the shrewd tactical skills of Brearley. While Botham led England, the Australians felt they had the edge . . . because their game was based on teamwork and it was apparent to Hughes and his men that Botham did not have the total support of the hard-bitten home professionals. The self-denial of Botham and the re-appearance of Brearley triggered a different response in both sides. England's professionals began to play with the vigour and enthusiasm of their youth and Botham found the form that had eluded him since he had taken over as leader in the 1980 home series against the West Indies.

Against Botham, the Australians had no answer. When he lashed 149 not out at Headingley and 118 at Manchester, bowlers of the class of Dennis Lillee, Terry Alderman and Ray Bright merely adopted the same tactics as before and hoped he would hit a catch somewhere in the outfield. Those tactics were probably wrong. Botham's great strength and the obvious enthusiasm he found in hitting through the arc cost Australia dearly – and in the interim dragged many more people through the gate as if England's success was merely to be expected after the euphoria of the Royal Wedding.

Just as importantly, big Bob Willis started bowling as fast as ever in his career – at a time when Australia's batsmen were thinking they could have a full season away from that sort of worry. Willis gave the tourists no peace . . . at Leeds, Birmingham, Manchester and in the first innings of the last Test at The Oval. After that, his stamina gave way, which was not surprising for a man of 32 who had had four operations on his knees. Willis, in fact, played as large a part in the Australian demise as anyone. At Headingley, he bowled as fiercely as possible on a wicket that suited, grabbing the vital wickets of Trevor Chappell, Kim Hughes, Graham Yallop and John Dyson on his way to career-best figures of eight for 43. After that, self-hypnotism and the support of crowds that had decided that 1981 was to be the year not only of the Wedding but also the Cricket, willed him on to produce speeds and fire that had the best of most of the Australian batsmen. There is no doubt, also, that Willis has a fine memory of the 1974-75 series in Australia when England's batsmen were reduced to fumbling wrecks by Lillee and Jeff Thomson, who delivered thunderbolts on surfaces that suited them admirably. In 1981, he took his revenge – especially against Graham Yallop. Until the second morning of the Sixth Test at The Oval, Willis, with his long, wobbly run-up and straight-chested action continued to bother the tourists.

Botham's influence on the series can never be over-played. After indifferent performances while he was captain in the first two Tests, he gave full vent to his talents while Brearley bothered about the finer points of leadership. Finesse has never been a Botham characteristic. When given the chance, however, he produced such performances that forever put the lie to the belief of senior Australian players that he could not perform at the highest level. In the end, both Brearley and Hughes agreed that the Somerset all-rounder had been the single difference between the sides. Margins of 18 runs (Third Test) and 29 runs (Fourth Test) at least indicated some proximity in ability.

But where Australia matched, if not overshadowed their opponents in bowling and fielding, they had no such hold in batting or all-round performance. An analysis of the touring party's weaknesses must be countered by words of their strength – pace bowling. The Western Australian pair, Dennis Lillee and Terry Alderman provided a stark contrast. Lillee, on his last tour of England, was well known for his pace, fire and belligerence. Alderman, on his first, was known for little. By the time the tour was over, Alderman, 25, had eclipsed by one Rodney Hogg's record of 41 wickets in a series against England. His economical action and willingness to bowl interminable spells of out and inswingers perpetually had the England batsmen in a state of disarray. As a slip fielder, he put down only one chance in six Tests. Lillee, stricken by viral pneumonia before the series began, took 39 wickets including a career best figure of seven for 89 in England's first innings at The Oval. Had he been more than 70 per cent fit for most of the tour, the result might have been different. As it was, he bowled with the enthusiasm of a man 10 years younger than his 32 years and twice as effectively. The loss of Lawson through injury during the Third Test and the unavailability of Hogg for much of the campaign meant that Hughes did not have an effective back-up fast bowler of class to keep pressure on England's batsmen. Such was the luck of England. There are no excuses . . . only an admission that more spirited batting might have changed an entire summer.

Peter McFarline,
The Age, Melbourne.

First Test

TRENT BRIDGE
18-21 JUNE 1981

9

England's Search for Fast Bowlers

If last year's Test match at Trent Bridge is an accurate guide, the already difficult task of the England selectors in finding fast bowlers for next Thursday's First Test against Australia, is likely to be complicated.

Last year the fast bowlers moved the ball about in the air and off the pitch throughout and England played only one spinner, Willey, who bowled seven overs in the match.

Thus four fast or fast-medium bowlers may again be needed which will make the present lack of good young ones felt even more acutely.

It is not hard to relate this shortage to the fact that the counties have been inclined in recent years to recruit many more overseas bowlers and pure batsmen than in the early days of instant registration.

What the selectors have in stock, as it were, are Botham who is not the bowler either in his action or results that he was two years ago, Willis who is bowling remarkably well considering his infirmities but is inevitably not the fiery youth of yesteryear, Hendrick and Dilley.

Of the last two, Dilley has done little this season, has not been fully fit and is short of bowling.

In the absence of more young rivals of Dilley's generation, it looks as if all these may be in the team to be announced on Sunday. Selectors do in fact tend to start a series favouring experience and there is something to be said for turning to young players when older ones have failed rather than vice versa.

Compared with the bowling, the selectors' other problems are relatively light and short-term. The search for someone to bat No. 3 goes on but there is at least a choice from such as Love, Randall, Larkins, and Tavare.

Larkins is in fine form, plays straighter than most, which is an attraction nowadays, and has a touch of class. Though he has not been successful in his previous five Test matches, he would not be the first to establish himself at the second or third attempt.

Emburey has not been at his best on the soft pitches of the past six weeks and if a spinner beside Willey is included in the 12 picked, I suppose it might be Miller who has been making runs.

Otherwise the team might be something like: Boycott, Gooch, Larkins, Gower, Gatting, Botham, Willey, Downton, Dilley, Willis and Hendrick.

Selectors Hopes for Stability Rest on Woolmer

England's 12 for Thursday's First Cornhill Test against Australia at Trent Bridge includes, as expected, all four of the faster bowlers who have played in recent series and, less predictably, Woolmer.

In the search for someone to add stability to the early batting, the selectors have thus come back to the same way of thinking as this time last year.

Woolmer played then in the first two Tests at Trent Bridge and Lord's before being discarded in favour of Wayne Larkins.

At Trent Bridge, after surviving the early chances which were being given freely in the prevailing conditions, he had certainly done nothing frivolous and batted 6hr 40min for 75.

VALUABLE RUNS

Valuable though the runs were in the context of a low scoring match in difficult going, this was presumably thought to be too much of a good thing in the long term if matches were to be won and the bowlers discouraged.

If Geoffrey Boycott was at his most obdurate – and on this occasion he too played an important part, batting five hours in the second innings for 75, more action was required at the other end. So, after Lord's, Woolmer dropped out.

However, the West Indian opposition last year was exceptional and it is a mistake to categorise batsmen as being either strokeless or adventurous with nothing in between.

Woolmer's three Test hundreds in 1975 and 1977 were all made against Australia and in his more fluent style he may well bring the calm and experience at No. 3 which has been lacking recently.

UNUSUAL CONDITIONS

In the sunless weather of the last seven weeks it would not have been surprising to find a repetition of last year's unusual conditions at Trent Bridge when the ball moved extravagantly throughout. A few days' sunshine may change that.

11

If, however, last year's policy is followed after a look at the pitch and weather, Emburey will be the 12th man, leaving Willis, Hendrick, Botham and Dilley to fire away in their various states of form and fitness.

It must be 5½ years now since Bob Willis was patched up for, it was estimated, three more years' Test cricket if he was lucky.

If a young fast bowler of equal ability were in sight, Willis would not be required now, but he is and it is a great tribute to his determination and resilience that he is playing in a Test match again. When he came home from Trinidad in February nothing seemed less likely.

One of the heartening developments in the West Indies was the way in which Paul Downton took his chance, finishing the tour with the staunchest of innings begun in a crisis against fiery fast bowling.

When I have seen him this season, he has done little wrong, · and it seems right that he should start a home series as the wicketkeeper in possession.

---

18 JUNE 1981

One-day Debacle is Gloomy Augury for England

It is not so much the loss of the Prudential series, after a sequence of wins in limited-over matches, which augurs badly for England in the Cornhill Test series which starts at Trent Bridge today, but the manner of the defeat.

The Australian bowling improved throughout the three matches, has room for further improvement and seems better suited than that of many visiting sides to the average English pitch.

The pitch here, on this historic ground with its wonderful atmosphere, looks flat and evenly grassed and is warmly recommended by one who made thousands of runs here, Reg Simpson.

Yet on a heavily overcast day yesterday when summer, despite all the optimistic forecasts, still seemed a long way off, it was hard not to remember that last year the ball swung and moved off the pitch to an unusual extent.

Then this was to the advantage of the England attack rather than of the faster West Indies bowlers and at noon on the fifth day England, for the only time in nine Test matches against the West Indies, were close to winning.

They lost in the end by only two wickets and four years ago when Australia were last here England won on a good pitch by seven wickets.

The difference is that Willis, Hendrick and Botham, who between them took 15 of the wickets both in 1977 and 1980, do not at the moment carry quite the same confidence; and Australia have turned up not only with Lillee, a tremendous bowler anywhere, but Hogg, Lawson and Alderman whose recent form suggests that they will bowl very well here.

PLAY WILL SUFFER

Australian bowlers unused to English conditions have not always produced their best here but with more cricket being played overseas by young players nowadays that does not apply so often.

The series beginning today will go down in history as the first in England to be of six Tests and also the first to have Sunday play (here, at Edgbaston and Old Trafford). That means dispensing with a rest day.

I suppose that Sunday play for financial reasons may be here to stay. I doubt if the experiment of doing without a rest day will be successful or deserves to be.

In more exhausting temperatures it has not been popular with players. A day in which to recover from minor injuries has been proved necessary in the past and even though the finances may benefit, I should think that in the long run the cricket will suffer.

One other experiment which was to have been made in this series, the enforced bowling of at least 100 overs in a day's play, has been rejected by the Australians.

Whether or not this was the right way to tackle the overrate problem, it was a genuine effort by the TCCB to stop the public, watching both in person and on television, from being done out of what can be the equivalent of an hour's cricket per day.

In other countries the sheer joy of watching their heroes plod back 45 paces in order to bowl fast at the opposition seems to outweigh any sense of deprivation in spectators, certainly in the West Indies.

Perhaps it does here, too, Perhaps the Board is out of date in wanting more action. But many people, not surprisingly, find the ever-decreasing overrate boring and alarming and the Board undoubtedly have a duty to go on trying to reverse the trend.

---

19 JUNE 1981

Gatting and Willis heroes as England recover well

England and Australian batsmen struggled in turn yesterday, much as England and the West Indies did at Trent Bridge last year, and at the end of the first day of the First Cornhill Test, England, having been put in, were on paper somewhat better placed.

Their innings had been coaxed up to 185 largely by an admirably-played innings of 52 by Mike Gatting after which Australia, in the last 100 minutes, lost four wickets for 33.

The ball moved about all day, frequently lifting awkwardly. Much clearly depends now on whether it goes on moving, as last year, or whether a spell of hot sunshine turns the pitch into a true, easy-paced one.

Yesterday Lillie and Alderman bowled just as well as was to be expected on it. What was less predictable on recent form was that Dilley, Willis and Hendrick would be even more awkward.

Willis's umpteenth comeback ended in triumph as he took his 200th Test wicket by bringing the fifth ball of the last over back to have Hughes lbw.

Lillee did the England innings no good early on, while Alderman, in his first Test, bowled the first 24 overs upwind from the Pavilion end, taking four wickets and upsetting the middle batting.

They were loyally served by their close catchers. Six of the first seven England wickets were taken by catches in the slips or gully. Nothing was missed.

England could not match that. The Australian innings was only four overs old when Dyson, before scoring, gave the sort of catch to second slip which had been sticking every time

14

earlier. This one, off Willis, popped out of Botham's hands. Happily it cost little.

ABSENCE OF SUN

Both sides left out their spinners, which in view of the continued absence of sun to dry out a well-grassed pitch was not surprising. England may have wanted to play Emburey, but perhaps because they lacked full confidence in the form and fitness of any three of their fast bowlers, decided against it.

Lillee's opening spell was a model of its type. Nothing was wasted, the batsman was forced to play at almost everything, and though Gooch pushed the ball about almost nonchalantly for 20 minutes, he met one in Lillee's third over which left him, bouncing generously and had him caught at first slip by Wood.

In his next over Lillee produced a ball which bounced still more to have Woolmer caught off the shoulder of the bat, also by Wood, this time head high.

At the other end Alderman first tended to be a shade too short, giving the batsmen time to take the bat away. But after 55 minutes, in which Boycott and Gower largely stabilised matters, he surprised Boycott, who, half-stopping a stroke, was smartly caught by Border at second slip.

At 67, in Lillee's second spell, Gower fell from grace, and, cutting at a ball too close to him, was caught by the more backward of two gullys.

Willey survived until lunch but was out soon afterwards, caught at second slip off Alderman. When Botham was bowled driving across a yorker in Alderman's 17th over, England were 96 for six.

There was a 40-minute respite while Downton battled solidly with Gatting against fast bowlers now joined for the first time by Lawson. Gatting played neatly off his legs on the few occasions when he was accommodated in that quarter, cut hard and safely, and, as he had from the first, saved himself a lot of trouble by a shrewd choice of when not to play.

He was batting with a secure look which nobody else approached all day, when, five minutes before tea, he signalled for a new glove, and, as if in a momentary lapse of concentration pulled in somewhat cavalier fashion at Hogg's next ball, which was shortish outside the off-stump. It bounced less than most and came in enough to flick the pad and have him lbw.

Willis was superbly caught first ball by Marsh wide down the legside, but Dilley, rotating furiously, despatched Hogg and

Lawson to some unlikely parts with some splendidly uncompli-
cated blows in an invaluable last-wicket stand of 26 with
Hendrick.

Within a few minutes Dilley, who has not exactly been
setting the Medway on fire this season, won further glory by
having the formidable Wood lbw second ball, and beating
Yallop more than once in his first over.

DYSON GOES

Dyson lasted an hour before Willis, now switched to the
down wind end, made a ball bounce to the glove or there-
abouts, whence it lobbed up to short leg.

Hendrick had now embarked on a spell which yielded only
four runs in his first seven overs, and in his next over Yallop
met a ball which bounced more than expected and was played
down on to the wicket.

After another half hour of playing and missing Willis brought
off his final coup, and England went in marvellously placed
considering their early suffering, owing much to Gatting but
also to the way in which their much maligned bowlers took
their chance.

The Scoreboard

England: First innings

		Bowling	O	M	R	W
G. A. Gooch, c Wood, b Lillee	10	Lillee	13	3	34	3
G. Boycott, c Border, b Alderman	27	Alderman	24	7	68	4
R. A. Woolmer, c Wood, b Lillee	0	Hogg	11.4	1	47	3
D. I. Gower, c Yallop, b Lillee	26	Lawson	8	3	25	0
M. W. Gatting, lbw, b Hogg	52					
P. Willey, c Border, b Alderman	10					
I. T. Botham, b Alderman	1					
P. R. Downton, c Yallop, b Alderman	8					
G. R. Dilley, b Hogg	34					
R. G. D. Willis, c Marsh, b Hogg	0					
M. Hendrick, not out	6					
Extras (lb 6, w 1, nb 4)	11					

Total 185

Fall of wickets: 1-13, 2-13, 3-57, 4-67,
  5-92, 6-96, 7-116, 8-159, 9-159.

Australia: First innings
G. M. Wood, lbw, b Dilley   0
J. Dyson, c Woolmer, b Willis   5
G. N. Yallop, b Hendrick   13
K. J. Hughes, lbw, b Willis   7
T. M. Chappell, not out   5
   Extras (lb 1, nb 2)   3

                    Total (4 wkts) 33
Fall of wickets: 1-0, 2-21, 3-21, 4-33.

Teams – First Test
England: Gooch, Boycott, Woolmer,
Gower, Gatting, Willey, Botham,
Downton, Dilley, Willis, Hendrick
Australia: Dyson, Wood, Yallop,
Hughes, Chappell, Border, Marsh,
Lawson, Lillee, Hogg, Alderman

Bowling	O	M	R	W
Dilley	5	2	8	1
Willis	10.5	6	12	2
Hendrick	9	4	10	1

Umpires: W. E. Alley and D. J. Constant

20 JUNE 1981

Fumbling England Allow Border to Rally Australia

England missed their catches, six by the kind-
liest count, and let Australia slip away yester-
day until at the end of the second day of the First Cornhill Test,
Australia's reply to England's 185 had been allowed to creep up
to 166 for nine.

Everyone needed luck to survive for long on this pitch and
England provided it for Allan Border by dropping him when he
was 10 and 17. They also missed Lillee early in his innings of
nearly an hour.

Thus Border, who came in at the start of a day's play twice
interrupted for long periods by drizzle, steered Australia on latterly with a look of security only achieved previously by Gatting.

He was still there with Alderman, the No. 11, when bad light
ended operations at two minutes to seven, having batted
throughout the three hours 55 minutes play.

All this must have been a bitter disappointment to England,
who, having taken four wickets for 33 overnight, bowled less
well than on Thursday, but well enough in gloomy, overcast
conditions to have Australia out for well under 100.

17

Whatever happened after that, a lead of 85 or more would have been a great help.

In the half-hour's play before drizzle set in in the morning the uneasy Chappell had Botham diving forward at second slip for a catch off Willis which barely carried. In the second session of 25 minutes the bowlers had a wet ball and the batsmen had fewer problems.

Thus when play started at four o'clock with a reasonable chance of continuing Australia had advanced by 18 runs to 51 for four. This would have been 51 for five if Border, cutting in Hendrick's first over, had not survived a straightforward chance to Downton.

Whereas the Australians' close catching had been immaculate, England made it look next to impossible, which with the ball moving as much as it was put them at a serious disadvantage, especially if a player of Border's calibre was let off.

Border, cutting again, gave another chance, this time off Willis, and was missed again by Botham above his head at second slip.

At 64 Hendrick finished off Chappell with no help required from anyone except the batsman who was aiming wide of mid-on at a good ball well up to him as his off-stump went out.

VIOLENT MARSH

On this sort of pitch sensible slogging has as good a chance of success as anything, because the ball is unlikely to go quietly into the slips off the edge of a violent bat.

In 20 minutes Marsh broke up the close field with some massive strokes to the on side and made 19 runs before he pulled Willis to a great height over long leg.

Boycott was underneath, and in the prevailing fallibility nobody can have fancied his chances, but he judged the awkward catch perfectly and held it.

Willis, whose performance in this match has been a great credit to surgeons, physiotherapists and of course his own spirit, gave way at last to Botham, whom Lawson, after playing Hendrick nicely off his legs for four drove conveniently into Gower's midriff at cover point.

MORE BLUNDERS

The safe holding of two catches away from the wicket did not, alas, presage better times in the slips, because Dilley at

18

third slip soon missed a catch from Lillee which if taken would have made the score 114 for eight.

This was off Botham who moved the ball as much as anyone with fair control at first. He found the edge again but the ball did not quite carry to Hendrick at second slip and by then Lillee was established in an important stand of 37 with Border.

At the other end Dilley hereabouts was too often off target to cause the same concern as the others, but did eventually produce a ball which was too good for Lillee and had him caught at the wicket. Hogg then chipped delicately to mid-wicket, leaving Alderman 20 minutes in which, off Botham, he gave the hitherto untested Gooch a chance to hold the first slip catch of the day – but with a familiar result.

The Scoreboard

England: First innings
185

Australia: First innings

		Bowling	O	M	R	W
G. M. Wood, lbw, b Dilley	0	Dilley	20	7	38	3
J. Dyson, c Woolmer, b Willis	5	Willis	26	12	38	3
G. N. Yallop, b Hendrick	13	Hendrick	20	7	43	2
K. J. Hughes, lbw, b Willis	7	Botham	13	3	32	1
T. M. Chappell, b Hendrick	17					
A. R. Border, not out	57	Umpires: W. Alley & D. J. Constant.				
R. W. Marsh, c Boycott, b Willis	19					
G. F. Lawson, c Gower, b Botham	14					
D. K. Lillee, c Downton, b Dilley	12					
R. M. Hogg, c Boycott b Dilley	0					
T. M. Alderman not out	7					
Extras (b 4, lb 6, w 1, nb 4)	15					

Total (9 wkts) 166

Fall of wickets 1-0, 2-21, 3-21, 4-33, 5-64, 6-89, 7-110, 8-147, 9-153.

22 JUNE 1981

England Lose by 4 Wickets: Botham Stays Captain

Australia won the First Cornhill Test 50 minutes after tea on the fourth day at Trent Bridge yesterday by four wickets. England left them needing only 132 to win and even on this unpredictable pitch, on which Gatting's and Border's were the only innings of over 40, that was not enough.

After their rather successful first day England might have got away with the fact that they bowled less well than Lillee and Alderman but they could not recover from Friday's surfeit of dropped catches.

The loss of a Test match which could have been won sometimes precipitates a change of captain if one has been in the offing, but last night Ian Botham was reappointed for the Lord's Test on Thursday week.

The outbreak of missed chances on Friday – among normally good catchers – lost the match and though that was not wholly Botham's fault, he was one of those who erred.

The selectors would have been justified in deducing that his concentration in this, as in other departments was suffering from holding the captaincy and that this was the moment to do something about it.

Willis bowled well in this match and now looks more likely than before to last out the series. I would have been inclined to let him take over and to give Botham a rest for the moment to see what that achieved.

ROBUST INNINGS

But the selectors decided on no change, perhaps in the hope that if they do decide on a change later, it may be for the long term and not as a temporary measure.

When Saturday's play ended three hours early, England, 100 on with six wickets down, had been put in a perilous position by more fine bowling by Lillee and Alderman and more splendid close catching.

The murk and heavy rain came at a good time for Australia. Lillee and Alderman were due for a rest and Botham was showing signs of playing the sort of robust innings which he played on this ground last year and which might in a short time have greatly complicated Australia's last innings task.

On a different type of morning yesterday, cool, clear and sunny, much obviously depended on Botham. But after one or two cleanly hit strokes he pushed out at Lillee and Border at second slip took a catch low to his left which was more difficult than most of those dropped by England.

Downton had already been lbw to a ball from Alderman which came back to him and Dilley, after bringing his tally of runs in a low scoring match up to 47 with a few violent swings, mis-hooked Alderman to the wicketkeeper.

When Willis sliced Lillee to a deep backward point England were still nearly 50 runs short of requiring Australia to make the biggest score of the match in the last innings.

GATTING'S CATCH

In just over an hour's batting before lunch Wood pushed Willis into short leg's hands after which Dyson and Yallop played and missed at Willis and Hendrick with the frequency which has prevailed throughout the match.

After lunch they pushed ahead steadily until at 40 Yallop edged Botham into the slips where a new tenant, Gatting, dived left and held two-handed one of the more difficult catches which had gone to those parts.

Thereafter England always had too few runs behind them to allow them real hopes of winning but they reduced the losing margin in what I imagine were Dilley's two best spells of the season.

Though the pitch was easing a little in the sun, he removed Hughes and Dyson at 77 and 80. In the second spell, at 122, he bowled Border with a ball which came back a lot between bat and pad, and in the same over had Marsh lbw.

ALDERMAN'S ACHIEVEMENT

If the match was a disappointment, not all the individual performances were.

Of the bowling of Terry Alderman, who took nine wickets in his first Test, Kim Hughes said: "We did not think in our wildest estimation that he would bowl as well as he has done here. We thought of him as a stock bowler."

This is presumably what he will be on other pitches.

Meanwhile, though he was probably most people's pick as Man of the Match, Tom Graveney gave the award to Dennis Lillee for the impact which he made on the match on the first morning.

21

The Scoreboard

England: First innings
185

Second innings:

G. A. Gooch, c Yallop b Lillee	6
G. Boycott, c Marsh, b Alderman	4
R. A. Woolmer, c Marsh b Alderman	0
D. I. Gower, c sub, b Lillee	28
M. W. Gatting, lbw, b Alderman	15
P. Willey, lbw, b Lillee	13
I. T. Botham, c Border, b Lillee	33
P. R. Downton, lbw, b Alderman	3
G. R. Dilley, c Marsh, b Alderman	13
R. G. D. Willis, c Chappell, b Lillee	1
M. Hendrick, not out	0
Extras (lb 8, nb 1)	9
Total 125.	

Fall of wickets: 1-12, 2-12, 3-13, 4-39,
5-61, 6-94, 7-109, 8-113, 9-125.

Bowling	O	M	R	W
Lillee	16.4	2	46	5
Alderman	19	3	62	5
Hogg	3	1	8	0

Australia: First innings
179

Second innings:

J. Dyson, c Downton, b Dilley	38
G. M. Wood, c Woolmer, b Willis	8
G. N. Yallop, c Gatting, b Botham	5
K. J. Hughes, lbw, b Dilley	22
T. M. Chappell, not out	20
A. R. Border, b Dilley	20
R. W. Marsh, lbw, b Dilley	0
G. F. Lawson, not out	6
Extras (b 1, lb 6, nb 6)	13
Total (6 wkts) 132	

Fall of wickets: 1-20, 2-40, 3-77, 4-80,
5-122, 6-122.

Bowling	O	M	R	W
Dilley	11.1	4	24	4
Willis	13	2	28	1
Hendrick	20	7	33	0
Botham	10	1	34	1

Umpires: W. E. Alley and D. J. Constant.

Australia won by four wickets.

Second Test

LORD'S

2-7 JULY 1981

England Recall Taylor: Reprieve for Woolmer

A different wicketkeeper, Bob Taylor for Paul Downton, is the only change in England's 12 for the Second Cornhill Test starting at Lord's on Thursday.

Otherwise, the selectors have acted on the principle that if a player is worth picking once, he is worth picking twice.

Downton was unlucky that the only catch he dropped was the costliest of all, but the change is probably prompted more by the fact that his taking of the ball throughout looked somewhat awkward and untidy.

That in itself does not constitute grounds for parting company, but it is wont to weaken confidence once a straightforward catch has been dropped.

Downton, at 24, is still a batsman of limitations, relying largely on guts and application. Greater fluency of stroke is required at the moment at No. 8, where he is needed to bat for England.

So who else? Those young wicketkeepers who bat better than Downton keep less well then he does, which has meant a return to one of the old hands, Bob Taylor 40 next month, or Alan Knott.

MAIDEN CENTURY

Of these, Taylor is reported as keeping the better and, though his maiden first-class hundred was only made earlier this month and at the end of a dead match, he has played a number of useful innings for England.

He has not had a lucky career and, as one of the most respected cricketers of his time, will be welcomed back. In a way justice has been done.

He last played for England in the Bombay Jubilee Test match early last year when he set up a Test record by taking 10 catches, most of them off the then all-conquering Ian Botham, and shared with Botham in a match-winning stand of 171.

He was left out at the beginning of last season, partly because some slight lessening in his ability was detected and partly because this was to be expected at his age. But he was technically well ahead of the younger ones tried subsequently.

EMBUREY'S CHANCE

Bob Woolmer survives after making a "pair" at Trent

Bridge. I imagine that any hesitation about picking him again –
at a time when Chris Tavare and others are waiting full of runs
– was not so much caused by two failures in difficult conditions
but by the fact that he was twice out around the off stump in a
not unpredictable way.

There will no doubt be a second change in the side which
actually plays, for a better balanced bowling side including
Emburey will be required at Lord's.

This will mean leaving out the enigma, Hendrick, who looks
a bowler of the highest class, beats the bat countless times, is
treated with great wariness by batsmen – but somehow takes
remarkably few wickets.

---

2 JULY 1981

England Call up Parker as Cover for Willey

Paul Parker was added to England's team of 12
yesterday for the Second Cornhill Test starting
at Lord's this morning in case a finger injured on Monday
prevents Peter Willey from playing.

If Parker, 25, plays, it will be his first Test after several years
of near-misses during which the selectors have been waiting for
him to fulfil the promise of his Cambridge days.

This season he has made many runs for Sussex and averages
63. He was presumably preferred to Tavare as he is better suited
to batting in the middle of the order. He is also just about the
best outfielder in England.

The likelihood is that this time he will be 12th man, because
Willey batted in the nets yesterday and even if the finger has not
quite recovered in time for him to bowl at the start of the
match, it is in the second innings that his bowling is most likely
to be needed.

LACK OF BOWLING

After last August's Centenary Test, a social success but
scarcely a feast of cricket, anyhow on the England side, the first
requirement now is for a spell of fine weather and an entertaining match.

Who will win it is swiftly dealt with. As stated often enough recently, I doubt if England at present have the bowling to win on good pitches.

Their best chance may have been, as last year, at Trent Bridge but they should bat well enough to earn a draw if the weather and pitch follow the pattern of other years.

GLOOMY HISTORY

Behind them lurks that gloomy piece of history which badly needs adjusting: England have only won a Lord's Test against Australia once this century – in 1934 when rain and Hedley Verity between them accounted for 18 wickets in a day.

Searching for reasons why England should hold their own in the next few days, one lights on the fact that this is Geoffrey Boycott's 100th Test. It will not have occurred to many that he might fail to make a hundred in it.

The only other cricketer to have played in 100 Tests set a precedent which is only partly encouraging. Colin Cowdrey certainly made a hundred on the great occasion, against Australia at Edgbaston in 1968, but having reached the 40s with a brilliant exhibition, he broke down and did the rest in acute pain and discomfort.

Boycott runner

If he had been a horse, he would have been put down long before he reached a hundred. He struggled on – with, by a quaint coincidence, Boycott to run for him.

Thus a Boycott hundred here would be a happy and appropriate event. So would another innings from Graham Gooch such as last year's 123 here which was all anyone could wish to see at the start of a Test match.

Gooch and David Gower are both in form. Given a splendid batting pitch at Leicester last weekend, they made more than 200 apiece in the match. There is, therefore, hope for the batting.

INSTANT REMEDIES

With commendable patriotic concern about the shortage of young English bowlers, readers have come forward with suggestions ranging from instant deportation of all overseas bowlers in county sides to the employment of the grunt as used, apparently effectively if not melodiously, in lawn tennis circles.

The advantage, however, must lie with Australia who,

despite the injury to Rodney Hogg whose tour future is now in doubt, can still take the field with three formidable fast bowlers in Lillee, and the younger Lawson and Alderman.

3 JULY 1981

Gatting Rallies England after Lawson Strikes

Engand emerged from the first day's play in the Second Cornhill Test with a score of 191 for four after being put in and losing 33 minutes in mid-afternoon through bad light.

This represented a stout performance by Australia and particularly their young fast bowler, Geoff Lawson, who took the first three wickets in a spell of 22 successive overs which cost 34 runs.

Not for the first time recently England's innings was revived by Mike Gatting, who came in after lunch when Bob Woolmer retired with a bruised nerve in the arm, and he was only out 10 minutes from the end.

The extra interval for bad light, which occurred perversely as the Queen and Prince Philip were about to arrive, was a help to the Australians in that it kept their three fast bowlers fresher, but they had their problems immediately after tea when one of the three, Alderman, had to retire.

This left Bright to bowl from the Nursery End, while Lillee and then Lawson again fired away downwind. Gatting and Willey held them off for an hour-and-a-half, without dominating but without suffering much inconvenience.

The day was ending more encouragingly for England, when Gatting played back to the left-arm spin of Bright, seemingly unconcerned whether the ball hit bat or pad – for Bright usually bowls from wide of the stumps.

The ball hit the pad and, on one of the less full-blooded Australian appeals, Gatting was lbw.

This stand had steadied an innings which had had a sticky patch earlier after being given a dashing start by Graham Gooch.

Gooch and Boycott were out before lunch, Woolmer was injured early in his 75-minute stay, and Gower, usually so fluent, was out of sorts on this occasion.

27

England, as expected, left out Hendrick and Parker. Bright, for the injured Hogg, was the only change in Australia's side.

Less predictable was Australia's decision to field, based presumably on the assumption that a good pitch might do more for their fast bowlers before it lost pace and that it was a cloudy day.

It was some time before the ball passed the bat, but it passed the field frequently as Gooch, in what promised to be a repeat of his spectacular innings against the West Indies here last year, cut and played firmly off his legs and made 44 out of 60.

Lillee, in his first seven overs, was hit for 35 runs and, with Boycott seemingly well established at the other end, Gooch carried the innings along swiftly and safely.

All went well until the faster Lawson replaced Lillee. In his second over Gooch mishooked a ball which may not have been quite short enough for the purpose and was caught at midwicket.

SLOW PROGRESS

This mishap occurred after 75 minutes at a quarter to one. No one would have thought then that by half past three England, for one reason and another, would have made only another 28 runs.

Boycott, whose appearance at the start of his 100th Test match had been the occasion for an enthusiastic reception, had pushed ones and twos and held out hopes that on this excellent pitch the centenary might in due course be marked in the best possible way.

Yet Lawson proved a rather more awkward proposition. Slightly out of position in Lawson's fourth over, Boycott, having batted 100 minutes – even if he had not made a hundred runs – edged a ball fast to second slip where Border knocked it up to Alderman at third slip.

GOWER BECALMED

Woolmer was clearly not helped by his blow on the left forearm from Lawson early on. Gower, is now less prone to indiscretions outside the off-stump, where much of the bowling to him was directed, and he made only one run in 45 minutes after lunch before the light faded.

Twenty minutes earlier, with the score on 83, Woolmer, having reached 13 with difficulty, decided that the time had come to retire. Whereupon the pugnacious Gatting came in and hooked his first ball from Lillee for four.

That was the limit of the action for some time. Under a large bank of cloud the light was fading enough to justify going off when bowlers as fast as Lillee and Lawson were in action.

When they returned, Gatting hooked Lawson off the top edge for four, raised the 100 with a more conventional cover drive off Lillee and generally accommodated himself when the length strayed.

Gower, by contrast, was out of touch and restrained, though his big escape when 11 was from being run out.

He was called and sent back when starting for a second run for Gatting's glance to long-leg.

His dive seemed too late to beat Lawson's fine throw to the wicketkeeper, but Marsh apparently broke the wicket fractionally before receiving the ball.

After tea and the presentation to the Queen and Prince Philip, Gower achieved the unlikely feat of driving two successive balls in the same over from different bowlers for four.

Alderman retired with a hamstring strain after bowling two balls and Lillee completed the over.

Gower, still not at his best, had been in for 30 overs when he played, without any marked adjustment of the feet, at Lawson, then in his 19th over, and was caught at the wicket.

Gatting, sweeping, driving and cutting, made nine runs off an over from Bright and passed his third fifty in successive Tests against Australia with two spectacular hooks off Lillee, before he succumbed.

The Scoreboard

England: First innings

G. A. Gooch, c Yallop, b Lawson	44
G. Boycott, c Alderman, b Lawson	17
R. A. Woolmer, retired hurt	13
D. J. Gower, c Marsh, b Lawson	27
M. W. Gatting, lbw, b Bright	59
P. Willey, not out	23
J. E. Emburey, not out	0
Extras (lb 2, nb 6)	8

Total (4 wkts) 191

Fall of wickets: 1-60, 2-65, 3-134, 4-187.

Bowling	O	M	R	W
Lillee	24.4	6	76	0
Alderman	13.2	1	38	0
Lawson	26	11	40	3
Bright	13	6	29	1

Teams – Second Test

England: Gooch, Boycott, Woolmer, Gower, Gatting, Botham, Willey, Dilley, Taylor, Emburey, Willis

Australia: Wood, Dyson, Yallop Hughes, Chappell, Border, Marsh, Bright, Lawson, Lillee, Alderman

Lawson Mops Up England's Tail after Willey's 82

The day's play which just about promised to overcome interruptions from the weather, ended in ill-humour yesterday evening when bad light halted operations at seven o'clock, with Australia's score 10 for no wicket in answer to England's 311.

The umpires, Ken Palmer and Don Oslear, were probably justified in coming off then with half an hour of an extended day's play remaining. Wood and Dyson had been playing Willis and Dilley with an uncertainty which could be attributed to poor light.

Within 10 minutes the sun emerged from behind a cloud. The umpires then went out to the middle but, though to the human eye the light was perfectly good, the light-meters apparently did not show the improved reading required.

So, the last 20 minutes' play was missed in passable light, and the crowd, not surprisingly sensitive about such matters after last year's Centenary Test, were infuriated to the extent of littering the outfield with cushions.

They get no sympathy for that. Neither do those who wanted light-meters and now do not like what the meters tell them. But the meters are intended as a guide not the last word.

It is a fair comment that, in view of last year's troubles and the fact that 99 minutes had already been lost from yesterday's play through rain, the umpires should have erred on the side of playing on.

LATE COLLAPSE

In all, play was reduced to just under four hours, in which an England fifth-wicket stand of 97 between Willey and Emburey was followed by the fall of the last six wickets for 27.

Most of those went to the young fast bowler, Geoff Lawson, who in a marvellously sustained exhibition on Thursday and yesterday bowled 43.1 overs and took seven wickets for 81.

If, as often seems certain, some mischievous imp directs the English climate – and with flair – he produced a little master-piece yesterday.

Noticing an unusually full ground, occupied by many more than the 23,000 of Thursday, he let the first of several showers fall after 15 minutes play.

When these ceased and the elaborate process of removing the

covers was underway, he first delayed it with a few more well-timed drops and then slipped in another shower as the umpires came out for a restart at 2.25.

So it was nearly a quarter to three before Willey and Emburey continued their stand, and not surprisingly – in view of the interruptions, fresh bowlers and, after four overs in the afternoon, the new ball – the batting was, at first, less than sparkling.

However, such luck as was going went to the batsmen. Emburey found a way through the slips, Willey acquired four runs over them, apparently off the back of the bat, when he aimed to glance Lillee and played too soon.

Alderman, when he relieved Lawson, was forced by his ham-string strain to bowl off a short run.

There were some things for which to be grateful. The sun came out, the drinks interval, taken in what the crowd thought were less than parched conditions, lacked the prolonged leisure of such interludes in the Orient, and Emburey was not a completely dormant nightwatchman.

Willey, too, began to play some fine strokes. Some fierce cutting and an off-drive off the back foot were interspersed with the nicking through the slips by both batsmen, which had a certain droll entertainment value for the crowd, if not for the Australians.

At 260 for four, the England innings was moving into relative prosperity when another shower arrived and most of the combatants went off.

Three Australians, presumably doubting the capabilities of the oncoming cloud, stayed out for a time, but tea could be taken and only another 20 minutes play was lost.

KEEN FIELDING

A wet ball, which required wiping, lowered the over rate still further, and England's progress at three runs an over, seemed less than it was. The slips were again bypassed more than once, usually when Alderman moved the ball off the pitch, and Willey, when 63, cut him hard through Border's hands at second slip.

Eventually the luck changed abruptly – or was changed by Border, who dived left in front of first-slip to catch Willey two-handed.

Fifteen minutes later Emburey went for a bold second run to long-leg, where Lillee had been spending the evening signing autographs.

For all their frustration, the Australians' fielding had been keen and athletic, and Lillee did his bit by throwing first bounce straight to Marsh before Emburey arrived.

Any idea that Emburey's departure, after three useful hours in support of Willey, would make way for an acceleration was not justified by events. Botham played across his third ball from Lawson and was lbw.

In the same over Taylor met one which lifted nastily to the glove and was well caught by Hughes hurling himself to his right at forward short-leg.

With a mishook by Woolmer and a catch to first slip by Willis, smartly picked up by Wood, the innings ended.

The Scoreboard

England: First innings

G. A. Gooch, c Yallop, b Lawson	44
G. Boycott, c Alderman, b Lawson	17
R. A. Woolmer, c Marsh, b Lawson	21
D. J. Gower, c Marsh, b Lawson	27
M. W. Gatting, lbw, b Bright	59
P. Willey, c Border, b Alderman	82
J. E. Emburey, run out	31
I. T. Botham, lbw. b Lawson	0
R. W. Taylor, c Hughes, b Lawson	0
G. R. Dilley, not out	1
R. G. D. Willis, c Wood, b Lawson	1
Extras (b 2, lb 3, w 3, nb 10)	18
Total	311

Fall of wickets: 1-60, 2-63, 3-134, 4-187, 5-284, 6-293, 7-293, 8-293, 9-298.

Bowling	O	M	R	W
Lillee	35.4	7	102	0
Alderman	30.2	7	79	1
Lawson	43.1	14	81	7
Bright	15	7	31	1

Australia: First innings

G. M. Wood, not out	5
J. Dyson, not out	3
Extras (b 1, nb 1)	2
Total (0 wkts)	10

Bowling	O	M	R	W
Willis	1.3	0	3	0
Dilley	1	0	5	0

Umpires: D. O. Oslear and K. E. Palmer.

England's Task is to Prevent Big Australian Lead

If England, with a new ball available this morning after four overs, are on even terms with Australia, who are still 58 runs behind with four wickets left, they owe it to three catches.

At present, Australia's most dangerous batsmen are usually Wood, Hughes, and Border. On Saturday they were all cut off when going well by brilliant catches by Taylor, Willis and Gatting respectively.

Thus this morning Australia are not in sight of the big lead which might, if augmented by early mishaps in England's second innings, have had England in grave difficulty in the last two days.

Let down by the slip catching though the bowlers were on the nightmare Friday at Trent Bridge when nothing stuck, they had no cause for complaint here.

The long-hop was greatly favoured and one lost count of the times when the Australian batsmen, always happy on the back foot, were cutting or hooking.

Certainly Lawson bowled a lot that was short while taking his seven wickets in the England innings but he is faster. So was the pitch then and errors were more likely.

RUN-UP PROBLEMS

Willis was the best of the England bowlers, but he had such problems with his run-up that he contributed 21 no-balls to the 47 extras which were the second top score.

So England looked rather less than a ruthlessly efficient machine in the field and the surprise was not that Australia recovered from a start of 81 for four, but that they made such a start.

For this Taylor's catching of Wood, who made 44 splendid runs out of the first 62 in an hour, was largely responsible. Changing direction, he hurled himself right to take the catch off the inside edge, Willis the bowler.

Gower took a straightforward catch with ease at second slip from Dyson off a good length ball from Botham. Yallop, tucked up, dragged a ball from Dilley down on to the stumps.

AWKWARD LIFT

The ball moved at times off the pitch before lunch and

33

occasionally lifted unexpectedly at the Nursery End. Taylor was out thus on Friday and just before lunch on Saturday, Chappell met an awkward one from Dilley which, though trying not to play, he touched to the wicketkeeper.

The weather, which had delayed the start for 35 minutes, was now pleasant enough and the afternoon passed agreeably, with partnerships of 86 and 77 and no real suggestion that England had the means to press home their advantage.

Emburey, when he came on at 167, had Hughes caught with his third ball by Willis, who backed away at deep mid-off and held the skier above his head as he toppled over. Students of form back Willis to hold this sort of catch where others more agile might fail.

Border went on with Marsh, now batting better than for some time, in support, but Botham forced Border to play too close to the body and Gatting at second slip took a marvellous two-handed catch to his left when the ball was almost past him.

UMPIRES' MISUNDERSTANDING

Thus neither side took a decisive advantage and it needs something exceptionally good or bad on one side in the next two days to avoid a draw.

Before play started Donald Carr, the secretary of the TCCB, issued a statement deeply regretting the "misunderstanding over the interpretation" of the regulations governing play in the extra hour on Friday when 15 minutes play was lost in evening sunshine through "bad light".

There will no doubt be a rigorous inquiry to discover not only how the mistakes came to be made, but how on this most sensitive of occasions, the Lord's Test, the considerable progress made this season – after last year's Centenary Test muddle – in relations between umpires, captains, ground authorities and the public, was not reflected here.

The Scoreboard

England: First innings
311

Australia: First innings

M. Wood, c Taylor, b Willis	44
J. Dyson, c Gower, b Botham	7
G. N. Yallop, b Dilley	1
K. J. Hughes, c Willis, b Emburey	42
T. M. Chappell, c Gatting, b Botham	64
R. W. Marsh, not out	43
R. J. Bright, not out	3
Extras (b 6, lb 11, w 4, nb 26)	47

Total (6 wkts) 253.

Bowling	O	M	R	W
Willis	16	4	33	1
Dilley	19	4	74	2
Botham	22	8	51	2
Gooch	10	4	28	0
Emburey	14	7	20	1

7 JULY 1981

Boycott & Gower Steer England Steadily Ahead

England's batting nowadays is less accident-prone than the bowling, which has not always been the case, and they finished the fourth day of the Second Cornhill Test at Lord's yesterday 95 runs ahead with only two wickets down.

Geoffrey Boycott playing in his 100th Test, and David Gower will continue their third-wicket stand, already worth 74, this morning.

Australia's first innings lead of 34 was just enough to cause concern, if they followed it up by making dents in England's batting early in the second innings.

Gooch was out just before the arrears were cleared off and Woolmer went when the lead was only 21, but for the last 1¾ hours Boycott and Gower carried out their unglamorous job successfully.

NOT ENOUGH

By then the crowd of 13,500 must have been increasingly reminded that though Australia may have a stronger, younger set of bowlers than England they have only four of them in this match – and that is not enough against efficient batting on a good pitch.

35

Boycott has batted for 3¼ hours with scarcely an uneasy moment and with plenty of encouragement for those expecting a hundred in his 100th Test today.

Gower has played very much in the responsible manner of the last year, with youthful dazzle replaced by mature application.

The hard truth was that, on this pitch, England would not reasonably be expected to bowl out Australia in the last innings today, but it was conceivable they might have run into trouble yesterday through carelessness or good bowling. That danger was averted by Gower, with a little luck, and Boycott.

ERRATIC DILLEY

England needed all morning and 35 minutes after lunch to take the last four Australian wickets for 92 runs. Dilley bowled a fuller length than on Saturday and he and Willis were unlucky in that a lot of playing and missing took place.

But much of the bowling was wide of the stumps and, for a time in Dilley's second spell, very wide.

Extras rose eventually to 55. In fairness it must be said that Willis, whose no balls (28 in all) made a useful contribution to that figure, has been firing away under the handicap of a chest infection.

The new ball had been taken after four overs and promptly brought the wicket of Marsh, who was surprised by a ball from Dilley which moved enough off the pitch to have him leg before playing no recognisable stroke. At 268 Willis brought a ball back to surprise Lawson.

So far the batsmen had been subdued and fallible but Bright and Lillee knew a long hop when they saw one and Botham in two overs was hooked and cut for four fours.

When the new ball was 17 overs old, Emburey came on to restore order and Bright, swinging towards mid-wicket, was leg before to him. For the rest of the innings Emburey bowled at one end and the last wicket stand of 31 between Lillee and Alderman occupied an hour.

Lillee picked up what runs he could and the lead grew very slowly, which was about all the comfort England could derive from the stand. To add to their frustration, Willey, pursuing a ball at long leg suffered a twinge in the hamstring and retired.

Eventually as the thinkers were advocating the yorker to dig out Alderman, Willis produced something entirely different which lifted awkwardly to touch the glove.

Gooch set the England innings off to a brisk start, albeit

without quite the authority of the first innings and all went well until Lawson came on after 40 minutes.

With his second ball he took his eighth wicket of the match as Gooch was leg before, playing perhaps a fraction late towards mid-on.

WOOLMER GOES

Woolmer lasted for 45 minutes before he was leg before to a full-length ball from Alderman. The fifth lbw decision of the day, in which only six wickets fell, must have been nearly followed by a sixth, for Gower, when three, went back to a ball from Lawson which kept low and survived one of the more confident appeals.

Boycott played very soundly and became increasingly busy when the left-arm spin of Bright was introduced.

Gower, by contrast, is wary of left-arm spinners and of the rough outside the left-hander's off-stump. After some rather hazardous slashing early on against the faster bowlers, he played Bright with much patience and with four or five fielders close to the bat.

It may be an encouragement to the bowler, but there are times when the opposite approach is more encouraging.

The Scoreboard

England: First innings

311

Second innings:

G. A. Gooch, lbw. b Lawson	20
G. Boycott, not out	47
R. A. Woolmer, lbw. b Alderman	9
D. I. Gower, not out	38
Extras (lb 4, nb 11)	15

Total (2 wkts) 129.

Fall of wickets: 1-31, 2-55.

Bowling	O	M	R	W
Lillee	11	3	35	0
Alderman	17	2	42	1
Lawson	10	3	20	1
Bright	12	7	17	0

Australia: First innings

G. M. Wood, c Taylor, b Willis	44
J. Dyson, c Gower, b Botham	7
G. N. Yallop, b Dilley	1
K. J. Hughes, c Willis, b Emburey	42
T. M. Chappell, c Taylor, b Dilley	2
A. R. Border, c Gatting, b Botham	64
R. W. Marsh, lbw, b Dilley	47
R. J. Bright, lbw, b Emburey	33
G. F. Lawson, lbw, b Willis	5
D. K. Lillee, not out	40
T. M. Alderman, c Taylor, b Willis	5
Extras (b 6, lb 11, w 6, nb 32)	55

Total 345.

Fall of wickets: 1-62, 2-62, 3-69, 4-81, 5-167, 6-244, 7-257, 8-268, 9-314.

Australia: First innings cont.

Bowling	O	M	R	W
Willis	27.4	9	50	3
Dilley	30	8	106	3
Botham	26	8	71	2
Gooch	10	4	28	0
Emburey	25	15	35	2

Umpires: D. O. Oslear and K. Palmer.

---

8 JULY 1981

Botham Resigns: Selectors May Recall Brearley

Ian Botham forestalled the England selectors at the end of the drawn Second Cornhill Test yesterday evening and told the chairman, Alec Bedser, that he thought it was not fair on the team or himself that he should continue as captain on a one match basis.

The selectors had already decided on a change and said that they could not agree to appoint him for the remaining four Tests. They will announce his successor today.

It seems highly probable that it will be his predecessor and mentor, Mike Brearley.

Mr Bedser stressed that Botham had in no way held a pistol to the selectors head. "He is not like that," he said. "The biggest factor in wanting a change is that we think it is affecting his form. The best way to find out if this is true is to see how he plays when relieved of responsibility."

BOWLED FIRST BALL

Botham completed a "pair" in the match yesterday when he was bowled first ball in a hectic piece of batting before his declaration. England, had, in fact, had a good day, finishing with the initiative and though not many problems were solved, at least the opposition was made to look less formidable.

If Brearley, 39, is the new captain, it would be unsatisfactory in that he would be occupying a place which would otherwise go to one of the younger developing batsmen and in that he is not available for India in November.

But he has been making runs and was a highly intelligent and respected England captain in good times and bad.

If appointed, he would give the selectors breathing space and a freer hand when they come to pick the captain for India.

However, the main importance of the change is that it gives Botham a chance to recover the form which is vital to any England side.

It was under Brearley that Botham prospered and it is one of England's current weaknesses not only that Botham has lost form but that there is no one in sight who might replace him as an all-rounder who affects the whole balance and strength of the side.

Yesterday morning Boycott and Gower extended their third wicket stand to 123 on a far from straightforward pitch. At lunch Gower was still there, the danger was over and in an admirably positive hour's batting afterwards 68 runs were scored in 16 overs for the loss of five wickets.

ATTACK HANDICAPPED

The declaration left Australia to make 232 in two hours 50 minutes or, as it proved, 51 overs. Before they could show whether they were interested in this proposition, they began losing wickets. After 15 overs they were 17 for three and happy to ward off further mishaps.

England for their part, were scarcely equipped to bowl them out in the absence of Willey with a hamstring strain. Willis and Dilley did well to take the first three wickets but there was only one spinner, Emburey, present. With a left-arm spinner to partner him (and quicken the over-rate) they might have embarrassed Australia still more.

For the fast bowlers the main hope lay in the odd ball which deviated or lifted. Bright, however, bowling over the wicket to both right and left-handers turned the ball a lot in the morning.

Whereas Gower had had to cope with him pitching in the rough on Monday evening, Boycott was mostly at his end yesterday. Boycott is seldom in trouble against spin on any pitch but on this occasion Bright turned the ball several times from around middle and leg past Boycott's bat and off stump amid agonised cries from the Australians.

It took an hour for Boycott to move from 47 to 50 and 20 of the 29 runs scored came from Gower who advanced with some cutting and carving through and over the slips but with textbook strokes as well.

Boycott eventually took 10 runs off an over which Lawson

bowled short outside the off-stump and then followed a ball from Lillee to be caught at the wicket.

Gower by now was playing some fine strokes, mostly off the back foot. When Bright for once strayed down the leg side, he pulled him for six over mid-wicket.

At lunch England's lead was 163 and the attack began immediately afterwards. Gower driving at Lillee, survived a huge skier to Hughes at deep mid-on, Gatting ran down the pitch to drive Bright for a magnificent long six at the Nursery End and then both were caught at slip off successive balls. Gatting succumbed to Bright off bat and pad, Gower to Lillee off one which lifted.

In the prevailing mood of adventure there were bound to be mishaps and Botham, denying himself any assessment of a variable pitch, pulled against the spin of his first ball from Bright and was bowled.

DILLEY PROMOTED

Dilley commendably was promoted to swing the bat which he did with success. Willey soon had Lillee bowling with four or five men on the boundary and then sliced him for six over cover-point.

Willey departed, having picked the wrong ball to assault, but Dilley carried on with some thumping pulls off Lillee, Taylor jumped out to pull Bright for six and when he was bowled, there were enough runs for a declaration.

Dyson was lbw to Dilley in the second over of the Australian innings and Yallop was neatly picked up by Botham at second slip off Willis in the ninth.

In the second over after tea Hughes played across a ball from Dilley, after which Chappell dug in for 65 minutes until the fifth over of the last hour. Wood had been close to being caught off bat and pad when four but he played well at one end and was still there when England gave up with two overs to go.

Lawson was made Man of the Match for his 7-81 in the first innings.

The Scoreboard

England: First innings
311
Second innings:

G. A. Gooch, lbw, b Lawson	20
G. Boycott, c Marsh, b Lillee	60
R. A. Woolmer, lbw, b Alderman	9
D. I. Gower, c Alderman, b Lillee	89
M. W. Gatting, c Wood, b Bright	16
I. T. Botham, b Bright	0
P. Willey, c Chappell, b Bright	12
G. R. Dilley, not out	27
R. W. Taylor, b Lillee	8
Extras (b 2, lb 8, nb 13)	23

Total (8 wkts dec.) 265.
Fall of wickets: 1-31, 2-55, 3-178, 4-217, 5-217, 6-217, 7-242, 8-265.

Bowling	O	M	R	W
Lillee	26.4	8	82	3
Alderman	17	2	42	1
Lawson	19	6	51	1
Bright	36	18	67	3

Australia: First innings
345
Second innings:

G. M. Wood, not out	62
J. Dyson, lbw, b Dilley	11
G. N. Yallop, c Botham, b Willis	3
K. J. Hughes, lbw, b Dilley	41
T. M. Chappell, c Taylor, b Botham	5
A. R. Border, not out	12
Extras (w 1, nb 2)	3

Total (4 wkts) 90.
Fall of wickets: 1-2, 2-11, 3-17, 4-62.

Bowling	O	M	R	W
Willis	12	3	35	1
Dilley	7.5	1	18	2
Emburey	21	10	24	0
Botham	8	3	10	1

Umpires: D. O. Oslear and K. E. Palmer.

Match Drawn

41

Third Test

HEADINGLEY
16-21 JULY 1981

Brearley can Help Botham Regain his Lost Form

The appointment of Mike Brearley yesterday as England captain for the next three Test matches at Headingley, Edgbaston and Old Trafford is better looked on not as the retrograde move which it might appear on the surface but as a holding operation.

The selectors have left themselves the final Test at the Oval, for which they can either reappoint Brearley or pick someone who, by then, they will have in mind as captain in India next winter.

Looking further ahead, one can foresee a much wider field of choice in a year or two when the present younger generation of England cricketers has more experience.

The choice then may well include Botham himself who in a stronger bowling side would not have as much on his plate. In the past 12 months to bat, bowl and field at second slip, where a high percentage of catches usually comes, was enough without the captaincy.

Botham's complaint, that a one-match appointment put too much of a strain on him and the team, has to be seen in the light of changing circumstances. Australia at home have seldom used any other method.

LESS OBVIOUS

The English system of inviting the captain first for several matches and co-opting him to help pick the team may have worked in the past when captains were old hands.

Now when the candidates for the job are less obvious, more numerous and younger and there are so many Test series, something nearer the Australian policy may be more appropriate.

In Botham's last match under Brearley's captaincy, that remarkable Jubilee Test in Bombay on the grassiest pitch which any visitor had seen in the Orient, he took 13 wickets and made 114.

I do not subscribe wholly to the view that he was greatly flattered by his results up until then. If not all his performances were against the strongest possible opposition, whose have been?

POWERFUL STRIKER

He was a powerful striker of the ball and, especially, a fine

44

fast-medium swing bowler with a splendid action.

His batting may return with practice and application. But the bowling, which was of a higher quality, is more important.

Whether his action was lost because of injury, because he is more heavily built now, or by chance, it is more likely to be recovered quickly under an experienced captain who handled him effectively in his great days.

13 JULY 1981

England Call up Old to Exploit Headingley Pitch

England have made only one other change apart from the replacement of Bob Woolmer by Mike Brearley, the new captain, for Thursday's Third Cornhill Test at Headingley. Chris Old comes into the 12 for Mike Hendrick.

Old seldom bowls badly anywhere, least of all at Headingley. The ball will sometimes swing there, and he will have been preferred to Hendrick because he swings it more.

He also keeps it well up to the bat, and, after the long hops of the first two Tests, the virtue of that has become even more apparent.

Recent Headingley Test matches have not been blessed by the weather and may be no guide to this one, but in one of the darkest and wettest of them, in 1978 against Pakistan, Old had the remarkable figures of 41.4-22-41-4.

Though Bob Willis, who had a chest infection during the Lord's Test, is not playing in Warwickshire's current match, that is just a precautionary measure. He will have a trial tomorrow, but is expected to be completely fit by Thursday.

Old's most recent Test match was the first of the series in the West Indies in February. It seemed after that that both he and Willis might have played their last Test, but their fitness this season and the shortage of obvious successors changed that.

USEFUL TRIAL

On the evidence of last week's match between a young TCCB XI and Sri Lanka at Trent Bridge that shortage may soon be ended. For once a trial or semi-trial produced useful information where it was needed.

The performance of Paul Allott, 24, of Lancashire, Paul Newman, 22 (Derbyshire) and Simon Hughes, 21, of Durham University and Middlesex, seems to have cheered everyone up. Among other things, they bowl straight.

The last two had only a handful of first class matches behind them, but good fast and fast-medium bowlers do arrive on the Test scene more quickly than other types. Bob Willis had played only half a season for Surrey before he went to Australia in 1970-71.

The dawning hope that the larder of fast bowlers might soon be not as bare as it has looked was not the only good thing to come out of the Trent Bridge match, for John Barclay's captaincy seems to have impressed everyone.

Though he played for Sussex in 1970, aged 16 while still at Eton, he may be one of those youthful prodigies who turn out to be slow developers at a higher level.

He will never want for keeness and, if his batting and bowling continue their steady improvement, there should be at least one English county captain for the selectors to consider in a year or two.

COUNTY TREND

In recent years, many counties have been led either by overseas players or by venerable Englishmen no longer in line for Test cricket.

Thoroughly worthy and sucessful though they may have been at the job, to England selectors in search of a relatively young English captain with some experience their appointments must have been bad news.

---

16 JULY 1981

Australia Growl about Brearley, Shirts and Subs

Before the Third Cornhill Test opens at Headingley this morning, on what looks a good drier-than-usual pitch, the splendidly trivial affair of

Dennis Lillee's shirt has to be cleared up.

The seeds of misunderstanding were sown yesterday when Kim Hughes, the Australian captain, proclaimed that the inference that Lillee was leaving the field after bowling to do anything else than change his shirt was an "insult" to Lillee.

Simple cricket-lovers will, of course, be horrified at the thought that Lillee might have spent the time not just changing his shirt, but having a shower, taking a rest, reading a coaching manual or receiving spiritual guidance.

In fact, nothing of the sort was suggested. When Lillee played in the Prudential Trophy, he had scarcely recovered from pneumonia and in the less formal one-day atmosphere, it was accepted that if he played, he would need to change after bowling.

However, he continued to leave the field after bowling in Test matches. So did England bowlers, for the practice has been spreading recently. In the West Indies, Croft was regularly coming and going.

BENNETT CONSULTED

Thus, last week Mike Brearley, on taking office again, mentioned to Donald Carr, secretary of the TCCB, that he thought that players leaving the field after bowling "made it a different game." Donald Carr consulted Fred Bennett, the Australian manager.

The objection was not that Lillee, or anyone else, was taking an unfair advantage, but that under Law 2 (1), he is not automatically entitled to a substitute if he goes off for reasons other than injury or illness. The consent of the opposing captain is needed.

No doubt this nice little brouhaha will be cleared up before the start of a match which will be contested by much the same sides as before but with a new England captain, a new electronic scoreboard and a new Test umpire in David Evans.

May all of them have a nice peaceful match, especially David Evans, a much respected umpire who kept wicket for Glamorgan in the late 1950s and has been on the first-class panel for 10 years.

England's performance improved during the Lord's Test and if, as is hoped, Botham's all-round contribution is the greater for being relieved of the captaincy, the difference between the bowling of the two sides on good pitches may not be as marked as seemed likely after Trent Bridge. Headingley has not been an

47

unlucky ground for England recently.

From a quick glance at page 380 of Bill Frindall's *Wisden Book of Cricket Records,* published today by Queen Anne Press (£14), I can reveal that whereas England did not beat Australia at Headingley until 1956, 57 years after their first meeting here, they have won three times more since then against Australia's one.

That is the good news for English eyes. The bad news is on the next page, the highest individual innings by an Australian in England, Bradman's 334 in 1930 and, also at Headingley, the highest fourth-wicket stand of the long series, the 388 of Ponsford and Bradman in 1934.

BOYCOTT & RHODES

This enlarged and up-to-date edition of an already monumental work is accompanied by *The Wisden Book of County Cricket* by Christopher Martin-Jenkins with statistics edited by Frank Warwick, also published by Queen Anne Press today at £11.95.

At the start of a Headingley Test, you are bound to look up the Yorkshire section and there you soon find that at the end of 1980 Geoffrey Boycott in 19 seasons had made 307 appearances for Yorkshire.

It is a quelling thought that at this rate he will not beat Wilfred Rhodes' 881 until the year 2017 when he will be 76. Even his prodigious stamina and patience may be tested.

17 JULY 1981

Dyson Celebrates after England Let Chance Slip

England dropped their catches at Headingley yesterday, as they did at Trent Bridge, so Australia were able to work their way into a strong position on the first day of the Third Cornhill Test.

John Dyson's previous highest score in 11 Test matches was 53, but, accumulating largely off the back foot, he batted doggedly for all but the last quarter-hour of the five hours 10 minutes' play.

His 102 steered Australia to a score of 203 for three, which in the prevailing conditions was good going.

Dyson was dropped at 57 and Chappell, his partner in a second-wicket stand of 94, was missed twice in the early stages of their two hours 40 minutes together.

England's bowlers were tidier than on many occasions recently and they were out of luck, but the bounce varied enough and the ball moved enough to suggest that this might be a pitch on which the Australian bowlers, with their extra pace, will prove a handful.

Nearly two hours' play was lost in the first part of the day, but the extra hour was played on an evening of brilliant sunshine.

LACK OF VARIETY

It was a fair guess that a three-week drought would end on the morning of a Test match, but one over was fitted in after a punctual start before the light faded for the first time. The players were soon back, but when it faded again, followed by heavy showers, the hold-up lasted for 35 minutes before lunch and 70 minutes afterwards.

Hughes had taken the unusual step of having another look at the pitch, after winning the toss, this time accompanied by Marsh, before he decided to bat.

Various factors probably created doubt, including the overcast weather in which the England bowlers were likely to be kept fresh by stoppages for bad light or rain.

England had somewhat surprisingly left out Emburey on a dry looking pitch with cracks in it. Such disappointment, which the lack of variety caused, was slightly relieved when the faster bowlers – Old, especially – kept the ball well up and generally made the batsmen work hard.

Just before rain ended the 65 minutes' play in the morning Botham bowled one over and brought his third ball back to have the left-handed Wood lbw.

In the afternoon Botham and Old bowled very well for an hour, moving the ball about and creating a new uncertainty. Only 11 runs were scored in the first half hour and Chappell, when three, survived a difficult chance off Botham to Gower diving left at third slip.

CHAPPELL DROPPED

Before tea Willey, who had a finger injury at Lord's and did not bowl there, had three overs but it was Willis off whom Chappell had his next escape, dropped by Botham.

It would be unrealistic to expect Botham to be instantly transformed now to the fairy prince for whom everything goes right.

He had certainly been running up more smoothly than for much of the last year, but when the first catch came his way at second slip, it hit him on the chest and bounced away. Chappell was then seven and the score 90.

With what seemed a reasonable piece of thinking, Brearley moved Gatting, who has been catching everything, to second slip and switched Botham to the gully. As if inspired by some impish fate, Dyson cut Dilley into the gully and Botham missed the catch two-handed to his left.

Occasionally Willey pitched short and was hit cleanly off the back foot, but batting became no easier as the unevenness of the bounce became more marked. Old, as the most accurate, caused the most uncertainty,

Eventually Chappell tried to force a ball from Willey off the back foot. It was probably not quite short enough for the purpose and he was caught at the wicket.

Hughes came in with 75 minutes left and was on hand to congratulate Dyson as he reached his priceless 100.

Dilley came on for a new spell and his first ball was of a good, full length. Dyson driving over and across it, was bowled.

The Scoreboard

Australia: First innings

J. Dyson, b Dilley	102
G. M. Wood, lbw, b Botham	34
T. M. Chappell, c Taylor, b Willey	27
K. J. Hughes, not out	24
R. J. Bright, not out	1
Extras (lb 5, w 2, nb 8)	15
Total (3 wkts)	203

To bat: G. N. Yallop, A. R. Border, R. W. Marsh, D. K. Lillee, G. F. Lawson, T. M. Alderman.

Fall of wickets: 1-55, 2-149, 3-196.

Bowling	O	M	R	W
Willis	16	4	44	0
Old	26	11	46	0
Dilley	13	3	39	1
Botham	13	4	33	1
Willey	11	2	24	1
Boycott	3	2	2	0

Umpires: B. J. Meyer & D. G. L. Evans.

Teams – Third Test
England: Boycott, Gooch, Brearley, Gower, Gatting, Willey, Botham, Taylor, Willis, Dilley, Old
Australia: Dyson, Wood, Chappell, Hughes, Bright, Yallop, Border, Marsh, Lawson, Lillee, Alderman

Botham 6-95 but Australians Grind on to 401

Australia took their score to 401 for nine on another interrupted day yesterday and declared in time to bowl for two overs at Boycott and Gooch – as it proved, without success.

For much of a day from which 50 minutes' play was lost despite the addition of the extra hour, Kim Hughes led Australia slowly on in a responsible innings of 89, which would have ended at 66 if England had not suffered another mishap in the slips.

Hughes and Yallop reached 332 for four with little other incident in a stand of 112 but Botham then removed both of them – and Border, Lawson and Marsh as well – in a splendid spell which had much of the old life and attack about it.

In 16.5 overs after tea he took these five wickets for 35, in all six for 95. It is the 15th time he has taken five wickets or more in a Test innings but, coincidence or not, it was the first time that he had done it since Bombay in February 1980, the last Test before he assumed the captaincy.

All that England had to be grateful for in the first half of the day was that the Australian score was growing only slowly and the reasons for that did no one much credit.

OUT OF REACH

Rain took 35 minutes out of the morning's play and another 75 minutes out of the afternoon and much of the bowling was not assaulted because it was out of the batsmen's reach.

The new ball was taken when available after three overs and Dilley fired it repeatedly well wide of the off stump. When he, at last, located the target, the surprise was too much for Bright who, having been hit by one ball in a painful place, was bowled by another.

Old was tidier and after bowling 31 overs, had yielded only 52 runs. Willis beat the bat but Hughes and Yallop continued their painstaking, if not exactly uncomfortable progress, with a gradual acceleration in the hour before tea.

GOOCH'S BLUNDER

Hughes played some handsome strokes through the covers off back foot and front. Yallop timed some straight drives well but at 3.30 p.m. the score had still only risen by 80 runs off the

51

30 overs bowled.

At this point Botham came on for a new spell and in his first over Hughes, playing forward, gave a catch to first slip which probably came slower than Gooch expected, Anyhow it bounced off his middle.

In the next over Old found the edge of Yallop's bat but though this time the ball was taken cleanly by Brearley, diving at third slip, it had not quite carried. It was that sort of day.

It was no comfort to England that the ball would still bounce unpredictably at times. Hughes had met one earlier from Willis which kicked shoulder-high from not much short of a length and half-an-hour after tea received one from Botham which came back to strike him in the area where Bright had been inconvenienced.

CAUGHT AND BOWLED

Botham's next ball was almost a half-volley and Hughes, playing it towards mid-on, lobbed it back to the bowler off the leading edge. He had batted in five separate pieces of play for 4½ hours.

There seemed a long way for the England bowlers still to go when Border, on arrival, drove Willis past mid-off for four with ominous confidence. But Botham was about to bring relief.

Though he damaged his right arm above the elbow in the field on Thursday, he had kept going pretty well, swinging the ball a little. At 354 he swung it in enough to have Border lbw while playing on the off side.

In Botham's next over Yallop cut, as he often had before, but this time the ball came back a little keeping low and he was caught at the wicket off the under edge.

LIGHT UNCERTAIN

With Marsh and Lawson together and an hour to go Australia had the ideal material for pressing on quickly, which they did for a time, though probably without much idea of bowling at England before the end. The light was too uncertain for that.

However, Botham made a ball lift to have Lawson caught off the handle and when he yorked Marsh, the sun was shining and Australia had the chance of bowling for 10 minutes.

The two overs were prolonged by no-balls and Gooch and Boycott came through them with one nasty moment when a near-unplayable ball from Alderman just passed the outside edge of Gooch's bat near the off stump.

The Scoreboard

Australia: First innings

J. Dyson, b Dilley	102
G. M. Wood, lbw b Botham	34
T. M. Chappell, c Taylor, b Willey	27
K. J. Hughes, c & b Botham	89
R. J. Bright, b Dilley	7
G. N. Yallop, c Taylor, b Botham	58
A. R. Border, lbw, b Botham	8
R. W. Marsh, b Botham	28
G. F. Lawson, c Taylor b Botham	13
D. K. Lillee, not out	3
Extras (b 4, lb 13, w 3, nb 12)	32
Total (9 wkts dec.)	401

Fall of wickets: 1-55, 2-149, 3-196, 4-220, 5-332, 6-354, 7-357, 8-396, 9-401.

Bowling	O	M	R	W
Willis	30	8	72	0
Old	43	14	91	0
Dilley	27	4	78	2
Botham	38.2	11	95	6
Willey	13	2	31	1
Boycott	3	2	2	0

England: First innings

G. A. Gooch, not out	2
G. Boycott, not out	0
Extras (b 1, w 1, nb 3)	5
Total (0 wkts)	7

Bowling	O	M	R	W
Lillee	1	0	1	0
Alderman	1	0	1	0

Umpires: B. J. Meyer & D. G. L. Evans.

20 JULY 1981

Contentious Rule Gives England Breathing Space

England's score of 174 on Saturday was not much below par for a diffficult course. The damage was done on Thursday and Friday when their bowlers allowed Australia to make 401 for nine.

The conditions were similar to those in which England, through the ages, have been wont to out-bowl visiting sides. Times have changed, and here it was Lillee (on his 32nd birthday) and his admirable young partners, Lawson and Alderman, who were in their element.

They were faster than England's bowlers. They bowled straighter, to a fuller length. And on a day when every batsman was likely to receive a lethal ball sooner or later, that was decisive.

Not all the slip catches were held but as more opportunities were created by the bowlers, that mattered less than it had during Australia's innings.

ANGRY SPECTATORS

England followed on 227 behind, Gooch completed the melancholy feat of being out twice in the four balls which he received during the day, the light faded under a bank of black cloud and the day ended in another bizarre outbreak of discontent at the playing conditions.

As at Lord's the trouble arose through the adding of an extra hour when more than an hour's play had been lost. It is ironical that this was instituted around 1974, to benefit spectators. All it has done here and at Lord's is to sour them.

Except during a brief return for four overs, the light did not improve and was still dim when five minutes before the original hour for the close of play, six o'clock, the umpires went out, consulted their meters and called off play for the day.

This was entirely in accord with the regulation which states that the extra hour will be played only if conditions are fit for play at the scheduled hour for finishing.

INFLEXIBLE RULE

They were not. But three minutes after six the sun was shining, the cloud was shifting, the crowd's wrath was rising. There was no room for flexibility because no captain is likely to agree to bending rules if his side might suffer by it.

The proviso has not previously given offence and has probably saved some fruitless waiting but it has been found wanting and will have to go.

England were thus given breathing space until today, though it is doubtful whether that will help them much. It would need the pitch to ease and lose pace under a hot sun, and that was notably lacking yesterday.

Gooch's departure, lbw while aiming at mid-wicket to the first ball he received on Saturday morning, will strengthen the lobby which thinks that ideally he would be more consistently effective further down the order.

The ball, from Alderman, may have started as if going down the leg-side but it moved enough to have hit the leg stump which, it is always likely to do when new, especially in these conditions.

54

Alderman moved an awkward ball away from Brearley for Marsh to catch him and Lawson bowled Boycott with an extraordinary one which came in from far outside the off stump.

There was a spirited stand of 42, by Gower and Gatting, each dropped once, but Gower touched a well pitched-up lifting ball from Lawson which Marsh caught above his head and Gatting met one which came back a lot.

The straight hitter had as good a chance as anyone and Botham, with some spectacular strokes, made 50 out of 75 in 75 minutes. But he tried too late to avoid a lifting ball from Lillee and Marsh took a catch which gave him 264 victims in Test matches, beating the record of Alan Knott.

He has done it in 71 Tests against Knott's 93, which reflects the quality of the bowlers, notably Lillee, to whom he has kept since 1970-71.

It is also a reflection of how cricket has changed and fast bowlers have taken over, that he stumped only 11 of his victims. His predecessor between the wars, Bertie Oldfield, out of 130, stumped 52.

The Scoreboard

Australia: First innings

401-9 dec.

England: First innings

G. A. Gooch, lbw, b Alderman	2
G. Boycott, b Lawson	12
J. M. Brearley, c Marsh, b Alderman	10
D. I. Gower, c Marsh, b Lawson	24
M. W. Gatting, lbw, b Lillee	15
P. Willey, b Lawson	8
I. T. Botham, c Marsh, b Lillee	50
R. W. Taylor, c Marsh, b Lillee	5
G. R. Dilley c&b Lillee	13
C. M. Old, c Border, b Alderman	0
R. G. D. Willis, not out	1
Extras (b 6, lb 11, w 6, nb 11)	34
Total	174

Fall of wickets: 1-12, 2-40, 3-42, 4-84, 5-87, 6-112, 7-148, 8-166, 9-167.

Bowling	O	M	R	W
Lillee	18.5	7	49	4
Alderman	19	4	59	3
Lawson	13	3	32	3

Second innings:

G. A. Gooch, c Alderman, b Lillee	0
G. Boycott, not out	0
J. M. Brearley, not out	4
Extras (nb 2)	2
Total (1 wkt)	6

Fall of wicket 1-0.

Bowling	O	M	R	W
Lillee	3.2	2	4	1
Alderman	2	2	0	0

Umpires: B. J. Meyer & D. G. L. Evans.

Botham's Magnificent Innings Brings England back to Life

E ngland were lifted off the ground in an extra-ordinary day's play in the Third Cornhill Test against Australia yesterday by the magnificent innings of 145 not out in 3½ hours by Ian Botham and by his stands with Dilley and Old who joined in flogging the three tiring Australian fast bowlers to all parts.

At 135 for seven, 35 minutes before tea, England were still 92 runs short of saving the innings defeat. But Botham and Dilley made 117 in 80 minutes for the eighth wicket; Botham and Old added another 67 in 55 minutes; and Australia, with the last wicket still to take, will need at least 125 in the last innings.

Botham's innings, following his 50 on Saturday and his six wickets, contained strokes which were classical, rugged and improvised, not all off the middle of the bat but hit with a power which forced seven Australian fielders to the boundary.

The devastation of it all is aptly shown by statistics. He reached 100 in only 87 balls and there was a period in which he made 64 runs between 39 and 103 by means of a six, 14 fours and two singles.

The pitch lost much of its unpredictability during the day but there was only half an hour to go when Hughes at last tried a fourth bowler, Bright.

By then Botham was down from a breakneck gallop to a controlled canter, and he lives on to resume his astonishing innings this morning.

EARLY WICKETS

In the first 65 minutes yesterday, while the ball was still new and Lillee and Alderman were fresh, three wickets were lost. Brearley reached forward to Lillee and was caught at third slip.

Gower took over half-an-hour to score his first run but, having made nine in an over from Lillee, played back to the first ball of Alderman's next over, which left him and had him caught at second slip. Gatting was lbw playing back to a ball from Alderman slanting in to him.

Willey stayed with Boycott for 55 minutes before lunch and afterwards glanced Lillee and cut him, also for four, in the same over. He followed with a fine cut off Lawson in the next over.

The first cut off Lillee was over the slips. Two overs later

Lillee dug in another short ball which lifted more steeply than most. Willey was cutting again and the ball flew straight to Dyson, newly placed for the catch two thirds of the way to the third man boundary.

Boycott held the other end safely for the first three and a half hours of the innings, missing little off his legs and seldom looking in trouble, even in the difficult first hour. Thus his departure, lbw to Alderman at 133, came as a nasty surprise, especially as he had taken a step forward to a full length ball.

Like Gatting earlier, he went off clearly of the opinion that the ball would have missed the leg stump, a view not shared by umpire Meyer.

Taylor soon pushed a ball to short leg which let in Dilley, master of the whirling slash square on the off side. With nearly all the strike he made 22 of the next 27 runs, shoving his front leg down the pitch and swinging the bat in a huge arc with either no contact at all or highly productive contact.

MASSIVE DRIVING

When Botham was 32, Bright, in the gully, stuck out his left hand but the ball was going too fast to hold. This and a hard chance to Marsh when 109 off a mishook were Botham's only escapes.

The main assault began with some superb strokes past cover point off the back foot, followed by cuts which were at the boundary before anyone moved, massive driving and a marvellous straight six off Alderman.

In half-an-hour after tea they made 36. Dilley reached his first Test 50 by flogging Lillee past extra cover and they were closing on England's best eighth wicket stand against Australia, the 124 of Hendren and Larwood in Brisbane in 1928-29, when Dilley at last swung at a straight one and missed.

Botham rushed through the nineties and passed 100 in two and a half hours with Old an active partner until Lawson yorked him.

Thereafter Botham kept Willis from the strike, hit the last few of his 24 fours with strokes of quality, surpassed his previous highest Test innings and ran off after playing one of the most memorable Test innings of modern times. In the two hours since tea he had made 106 out of 175 off 27 overs.

The Scoreboard

Australia: First innings
401-9 dec.

England: First innings
174

Second innings:

G. A. Gooch, c Alderman, b Lillee	0
G. Boycott, lbw, b Alderman	46
J. M. Brearley, c Alderman, b Lillee	14
D. I. Gower, c Border, b Alderman	9
M. W. Gatting, lbw, b Alderman	1
P. Willey, c Dyson, b Lillee	33
I. T. Botham, not out	145
R. W. Taylor, c Bright, b Alderman	1
G. R. Dilley, b Alderman	56
C. M. Old, b Lawson	29
R. G. D. Willis, not out	1
Extras (b 5, lb 3, w 3, nb 5)	16

Total (9 wkts) 351

Fall of wickets: 1-0, 2-18, 3-37, 4-41,
5-105, 6-133, 7-135, 8-252, 9-319.

Bowling	O	M	R	W
Lillee	24	6	93	3
Alderman	34	6	131	5
Lawson	23	4	96	1
Bright	4	0	15	0

Umpires: B. J. Meyer & D. G. L. Evans.

22 JULY 1981

Willis Achieves Unbelievable with 8 for 43

Just occasionally in life the unbelievable does happen. It happened on the last day of the Third Cornhill Test at Headingley yesterday when England, who had seemingly been within a few minutes of defeat on Monday afternoon with Ladbrokes offering 500-1 against them, bowled out Australia for 111 to win by 18 runs.

Ian Botham hauled them up from the depths on Monday and, having made 149 not out, took the first wicket when Australia batted yesterday.

But the 130 which Australia needed was very little on a pitch still producing the unpredictable ball but no more often than when they were making 401 in the first innings. At 56 for one indeed Australia seemed to be cruising home.

Then Bob Willis, having switched to the Kirkstall Lane end,

began to bowl as straight and as fast as at any time in the long career which has been miraculously extended after injury. He has only once produced better figures than eight for 43, but that was not in a Test match.

His inspired spell began 20 minutes before lunch when he took the first of three wickets in 11 balls. It ended 70 minutes after lunch when he knocked out Bright's middle stump and England incredibly had levelled the series.

COOL BREARLEY

The inspiration was not confined to Willis, for England threw themselves frantically about the field and, until the last few seconds, held all their catches, the best of them one by Botham and two by the agile Gatting while Brearley conducted operations with the unflappability which has coped successfully with numerous tight, limited over finishes in the past.

Twenty-four hours earlier England were 135 for seven, still needing 92 to avoid an innings defeat, and a few prescient clients were subscribing £52 to Ladbrokes. They have won between them £26,000.

Only once in more than 100 years of Test matches has a side following on been victorious: England won by 10 runs in Sydney in 1894-95. That makes this an extraordinary feat, but it is more extraordinary still to win from the sort of situation in which England found themselves before Botham and Dilley took over.

England's innings lasted another 10 minutes yesterday morning before Willis was well caught at second slip by Border in Alderman's second over with the new ball. Botham had driven Alderman handsomely past cover in his first over and five runs had been added.

NINE FOR ALDERMAN

The last wicket stand had made 37 in 31 minutes during which Willis received nine balls. The last three wickets had added 221 and, as at Trent Bridge, Alderman, who had not played in a Test before this series, had taken nine wickets in the match.

The only conceivable reasons then that one could find why Australia should not make 130 were conditions in which the ball might start to swing, a bad start which might lead to panic – or a brilliant piece of bowling.

Yet, on a lovely fresh sunny morning, the new ball swung

little and the Australians set off as if the task was trifling, Wood hitting Botham's first two balls for four.

In Botham's second over Wood drove and apparently hit ground and ball at the same time, Taylor taking the catch. The score than advanced uneventfully to 56 before Willis, in the second over after changing ends, made a ball lift and lob up from the handle of Chappell's bat.

Hughes played a form of steer towards third man fairly profitably in the first innings but now he met a ball from Willis which lifted more than expected and Botham dived at third slip to catch him two-handed to the left.

Yallop fended off a ball towards Gatting, a close short-leg. Gatting instinctively was back on his heels but recovered to scoop the ball up near his toes.

At that, they went in for lunch with the score 58 for four and an England win suddenly in sight if the inspiration could be sustained afterwards.

Willis, running in downhill, tended to overstep and the fear was that his rhythm might be upset by concern about giving away a dozen runs in no-balls. He brushed this aside to such an extent that in 32 balls he took six wickets for eight runs.

BORDER DEPARTS

The first wicket after lunch was the valuable one of Border. Old brought a ball back to knock out his leg stump off the inside edge.

In Willis's next over Dyson, hooking, was caught at the wicket. In his next Marsh hooked off the top edge and Dilley, backing downhill just inside the long leg boundary, had an unenviable catch but everthing was coming off now and he held it safely chest high. In Willis's following over Lawson touched a wide one to Taylor and Australia were 75 for eight.

Hereabouts it looked as if Australia had decided that the way to play was to hit straight and often as Botham had done. In Bright and Lillee they had two experienced cricketers to put this into effect.

BRAVE STROKES

Lillee dabbed Willis over the slips for four, Bright pulled Old twice in an over for four. Lillee cut Willis twice more for four. In four overs 35 runs were made and the match was slipping away again when Lillee miscued a stroke off his legs.

Gatting at mid-on had to move fast to reach a ball never very high but he hurled himself forward and caught it.

For Bright, Brearley now chose a field with two slips and the rest spread round the boundary. Botham had replaced Old and, after a leg-bye, had Alderman twice dropped in three balls by Old at third slip, the first chance sharp but straight, the second low and left-handed.

Mercifully it did not matter. For his next ball Willis produced a yorker, Bright drove over it and a never to be forgotten Test match was won and lost.

The Scoreboard

Australia: First innings
401-9 dec.

Second innings:

J. Dyson, c Taylor, b Willis	34
G. M. Wood, c Taylor, b Botham	10
T. M. Chappell, c Taylor, b Willis	8
K. J. Hughes, c Botham, b Willis	0
G. N. Yallop, c Gatting, b Willis	0
A. R. Border, b Old	0
R. W. Marsh, c Dilley, b Willis	4
R. J. Bright, b Willis	19
G. F. Lawson, c Taylor, b Willis	1
D. K. Lillee, c Gatting, b Willis	17
T. M. Alderman, not out	0
Extras (lb3, w1, nb14)	18
Total	111

Fall of wickets: 1-13, 2-56, 3-58, 4-58, 5-65, 6-68, 7-74, 8-75, 9-110.

Bowling	O	M	R	W
Botham	7	3	14	1
Dilley	20	11	0	0
Willis	15.1	3	43	8
Old	9	1	21	1
Willey	3	1	4	0

England: First innings
174

Second Innings:

G. A. Gooch, c Alderman b Lillee	0
G. Boycott, lbw, b Alderman	46
J. M. Brearley, c Alderman b Lillee	14
D. I. Gower, c Border b Alderman	9
M. W. Gatting, lbw, b Alderman	1
P. Willey, c Dyson, b Lillee	33
I. T. Botham, not out	149
R. W. Taylor, c Bright b Alderman	1
G. R. Dilley, b Alderman	56
C. M. Old, b Lawson	29
R. G. D. Willis, c Border, b Alderman	2
Extras (b 5, lb 3, w 3, nb 5)	16
Total	356

Fall of wickets: 1-0, 2-18, 3-37, 4-41, 5-105, 6-133; 7-135; 8-252, 9-319

Bowling	O	M	R	W
Lillee	25	6	94	3
Alderman	35.3	6	135	6
Lawson	23	4	96	1
Bright	4	0	15	0

Man of the Match; I.T. Botham.
Umpires: B. J. Meyer & D. G. L. Evans.

England won by 18 runs

Spirit of Adventure Returns to Cricket

England's staggering victory yesterday was not only a breath of fresh air in that it was unexpected but in that it was achieved in the grand manner by a spirit of adventure.

Among England's batsmen only Jessop's famous hundred at the Oval in 1902 occupied fewer balls than Botham's, 75 against 87.

Botham's innings no doubt will be remembered in 80 years time as an example of how they used to play in the old days, just as Jessop's is now. In that the new generation of young – unusually young – English batsmen are full of strokes and indeed sometimes err on the side of adventure this may not be an isolated case in the 1980s of attack being rewarded.

It was also a great match for the statisticians who do so much to keep Test matches in the minds of later generations. Almost unnoticed amid yesterday's excitement and other figures, Bob Taylor with the last of his four catches passed John Murray's world record of 1,270.

Headingley has shown that Test matches can still be won by the buccaneer. Yet in the selection of teams the buccanering, if any, was on the Australian side.

DRY WICKET

Seeing this dry pitch they included a spinner, Bright, instead of Hogg and played three fast bowlers against England's four, a decision which the purists would say was to their credit.

In the event it may have cost them the match, for if Hogg had played the pressure might have been taken off the other three whom Botham, Dilley and Old flogged so unmercifully in their weariness on Monday evening.

To that extent joy has to be restrained. Nothing has been done to bring back balanced sides or to restore the art of spin bowling to its place at the highest level of cricket.

But it is a good thing for any side to end a run of failures and to pluck victory spectacularly from defeat. In a season which has not been exactly one of golden weather and golden cricket the reminder that the sustained excitement of a really good Test match outdoes anything that limited over cricket can provide must be a boost for the game.

There may have been a tendency in the light of after events to underestimate the vital part played in England's revival by Graham Dilley, especially as he lost form and fitness and took no further part in the series.

When he came in soon after three o'clock on the fourth afternoon and struck the first blows in the match-turning partnership with Botham, no one could have foreseen that less than 24 hours later, victory would have been won and some of those most closely concerned would be saying what they thought about it all.

Mike Brearley: "Botham's innings was the most marvellous I have seen. He gave us our lifeline. We all went out there feeling we had a chance and Bob Willis bowled an inspired spell on that wicket."

HUGHES DISAPPOINTED

Kim Hughes said: "We are terribly disappointed that we have blown this game. We played badly in two sessions only and paid for it. But this is not the time to panic. I would like to think that England still have their share of problems.

"But there was simply nothing we could do about Botham yesterday. He took us apart. And there was nothing we could do about Willis today.

"The wicket was far too loaded in favour of the medium pacer and fast bowler. In fact the pitches in the three Tests have not been suitable for first-class cricket in my opinion. Still, the great thing was that people enjoyed the game. It was good for cricket."

Bob Willis said: "I don't think Nottingham or Leeds were up to standard. In this match, if the cracks were hit, the ball either squatted or went vertical.

"I bowled a lot of no-balls but the captain told me not to worry about it. We needed this win and perhaps the tide has turned for us.

"Mind you, when I was on the plane home from the West Indies for my knee operation, I thought I would never play any cricket again."

Sydney, 1894 – The Only Parallel

The First Test at Sydney in 1894/5 provides the only parallel with England's miraculous victory at Headingley in the Third Test of this summer's Test series in that of the 245 matches played between the countries it is the only other which has been won by a side following on. Though the two have been concerned in even tighter finishes the matches invite comparison also since the margin of success was so slender – 10 runs at Sydney in 1894, 18 at Headingley in 1981. Likewise each of these games provided the spark that set the respective series alight.

When A. E. Stoddart took a strong side out to Australia in the autumn of 1894 their early form was so sketchy that they were given little chance of success; even less, clearly, when Australia on winning the toss rattled up 586, which was then and for many years afterwards the highest total ever made. England responded with 325, whereupon with an advantage of 261 J. McC. Blackham, Australia's patriarchal captain and wicketkeeper, invited them to bat again.

Now with a worthy but not otherwise outstanding Lancashireman, Albert Ward, leading the way with 117 (to add to his top score of 75 in the first innings) and all but one man making double figures England reached 437, so leaving Australia 177 to win.

This was a stroke of ill-luck for Australia, but there is a moral attached to their second innings, for despite the uncertain weather they batted over-cautiously and with eight wickets left still needed another 64 runs when the fifth day ended. H. S. Altham records how next morning George Giffen, Australia's great all-rounder, was greeted by Blackham "with a face as long as a coffee-pot." Although the sun was shining it had rained heavily in the night, and Briggs and Peel, the slow left-armers, had a sticky pitch to bowl on.

Peel, having thought the cause lost and having enjoyed his evening out so thoroughly that he presumably failed to notice the rain, on arriving at the ground was put under a cold shower by captain's orders, and sobered up sufficiently to bring his bag to six for 67, Briggs accounting for the rest. 10 runs was the margin, and a Homeric series, won by England in the Fifth and final Test, had been put in train.

E. W. Swanton

64

Fourth Test

EDGBASTON

30 JULY – 2 AUGUST 1981

All Signs Point to Emburey

Eengland have picked the same 12 for the Fourth Cornhill Test, starting on Thursday, though if the Edgbaston pitch is anything like its predecessors of recent years, John Emburey will not be left out this time.

It is also intended to change the batting order. Gooch's somewhat statuesque operations against the new ball at Headingley revived the theory, of which Ken Barrington was a great advocate, that his power and freedom of stroke would be more effective further down.

Brearley will open with Boycott. Gower will move up to No. 3, making way for Gooch at No. 4. Otherwise the selectors have left well alone after last week's singular events.

On the evidence up to Monday lunchtime, they would surely have been forced to do something about the bowling which had been mainly responsible, with Australia's dogged and, as their captain admits, lucky batting, for building up an apparently invincible position.

Yet Edgbaston, with its record of true, mild pitches, is clearly not the ground on which to bring in inexperienced, untried fast bowlers.

IMPORTANT JOB

For the moment, experiment could be delayed. The selectors could retain Old who did an important job in the hour after lunch on Tuesday while Willis was working his wonders at the other end.

They did not have to rely solely on past evidence that Old could sometimes swing the ball at Edgbaston, where in 1978 he took four wickets in five balls against Pakistan.

They did not have to discard Dilley whose vital part in starting the revival at Headingley tended to be overshadowed by susequent events. I suppose, however, that he may be the one to make room for Emburey.

I doubt if the selectors would have left out Willis, the Warwickshire captain, at Edgbaston anyhow, and that he can still bowl as he did last Tuesday was probably not a total surprise to the chairman of selectors, who last week described him "as a permanent example of sheer hard work."

Dilley & Lawson Out: Edgbaston Set for Draw

Australia start the Fourth Cornhill Test match at Edgbaston today without their young fast bowler, Geoff Lawson, who has a back injury. He might well be badly missed.

In the Second Test at Lord's, Lawson took seven for 81 in the first innings, and he had a lot to do with Australia's victory in the Prudential Trophy match on this ground last month, making 29 not out and taking three for 42 in his 11 overs.

If, as seems likely, this well grassed but dry pitch is as mild and true as most Edgbaston Test pitches in recent years, the loss of a strong young bowler who can bang the ball in and occasionally achieve some unexpected bounce, is a bad blow.

Australia are lucky to have in reserve Rodney Hogg, who was bowling well early in the tour before he was injured. It is probable that they will make another change, bringing in Martin Kent instead of Trevor Chappell.

It will be Kent's first Test but he has been on the fringe of the Australian side for several years. He is the type of forthright, hard-driving strokeplayer who can give a bad time to bowlers struggling on an unhelpful pitch.

Graham Dilley has thrown his arm out and Mike Hendrick was added to the England 12 at the nets yesterday. But even before this it looked as if Dilley would be left out in favour of John Emburey who will doubtless do a lot of bowling.

This would be the only change from the side which at Headingley last week had gained the sort of victory unlikely to occur again in a lifetime.

On all the evidence this will be a very different match – on a pitch which should soon restore any confidence which the Australian batsmen may have lost on the momentous last day at Headingley.

In last month's Prudential match at Edgbaston which Australia won by two runs, nearly 500 runs were scored. In last August's it was nearly 600 and England in their 55 overs made 320 for eight.

When a Test match was last played on this ground, against India in 1979, England scored 633 for five. Boycott made 155, Gooch 83 and Gower 200 not out.

67

DRYING WICKET

Certainly when Australia last played in Birmingham in 1975, they won, but England batted on a pitch drying after a storm, which is not going to happen now that pitches are covered.

That was one of only five Test matches played between England and Australia at Edgbaston. The first two, in 1902 and 1909, bore little resemblance to those of modern times and in 1902 Australia were bowled out, in a drawn match, by Rhodes and Hirst for 36, still their lowest Test score.

In 1909 Hirst and Blythe bowled out Australia twice and England won by 10 wickets.

It was 1961 before Australia played an Edgbaston Test match again. They drew then and, after rain, they drew again in 1968. A draw seems the most likely result this time, too.

31 JULY 1981

Old Hits Back to Salvage Some Pride for England

Nothing could be quite as unexpected as England's recovery at Headingley, but in ordinary times an Edgbaston pitch on which England were bowled out for 189 and finished by taking two Australian wickets for 19 would qualify as pretty remarkable.

The ball moved a little off the pitch all day in this Fourth Cornhill Test, and the bowlers performed better than the batsmen, notably Terry Alderman for Australia and Chris Old in his five overs for England.

On a superb, cloudless day, England batted almost as if they foresaw easy runs ahead, playing strokes which were more suited to the ideal than the reality.

PROBLEMS FOR AUSTRALIA

Even allowing for the admirable steadiness and adaptability of the Australian bowling, they found ways of getting out which are unlikely to figure prominently in their autobiographies.

Yet Australia, with 50 minutes' batting, were soon having their problems, too, for Old, as usual, bowled the full length required.

In a fine second over he brought a ball back sharply to bowl Dyson and, in his fifth, he moved one away to have Border caught at the wicket. The day ended with honours even and the future obscure.

England's morning was much worse than could have been generally foreseen when they chose to bat. It was predictable that the new ball would move a little before lunch and Alderman, especially, would need treating with caution.

But the comfortable bounce was also predictable and it was reasonable to expect that, after a morning of judicious reconnaissance, a hot afternoon during which the bowlers would tire would be spent profitably.

For 45 minutes the action followed the script. At 29, however, Boycott, untypically following a wide ball from Alderman leaving him, touched it to the wicketkeeper. In Alderman's next over Gower aimed to pull a shortish ball.

He has played the same stroke frequently in the past, early as well as later in an innings, but this time he mishit and gave a gentle catch to a wide mid-on.

Immediately, England had two other nasty moments. Gooch survived a loud appeal for leg before, when Hogg brought a ball back to hit him a little too high, and Alderman found the edge of Brearley's bat whence the ball flew fractionally short of first slip.

GOOCH GOES

The communiqué of the umpires after consultation stated that Wood had picked up the ball on the half-volley, which does happen without the catcher knowing.

Brearley, having scored 13, spent more than an hour without scoring but with only a third of the strike. He became more active in the half-hour before lunch, and Gooch was playing well enough with him to suggest that the early mishaps would be rectified.

10 minutes before lunch, Alderman came off, having taken two for nine in 11 overs. Bright replaced him, and in his first over, Gooch, hitting hard off the back foot at a ball probably a little close to the body for this exercise, was caught at the wicket off the under edge.

Timing was not easy and after lunch the half-volley still did not go off the middle of the bat but for 50 minutes Brearley with most of the strike, played some good strokes on the off side.

Yet the ball still moved enough to require a full measure of footwork and when, at 101, Brearley drove at Lillee with the left leg not in the recommended district he was caught at second slip.

Gatting's innings was now blossoming but, having driven Lillee very hard past coverpoint, he drove again in Lillee's next over. This time he was not quite across to a ball slanting away from him and Alderman, at third slip, held a fast moving catch.

EFFECTIVE LILLEE

Lillee was relatively medium paced but no less effective for that. Bright, who came on again at the Pavilion End with his left-arm spin, bowled over the wicket with nothing much to hope for than some error if he pitched in the rough outside the batsman's leg stump.

At 145 he hit the target and Willey, aiming a half-sweep, was bowled behind his legs by a ball which came in a lot.

Botham played a cut over the slips and a lofted on-drive which must have revived awful memories of Headingley for the Australian bowlers. But in one over Alderman brought a ball back to bowl him between bat and pad and then, two balls later, bowled Taylor.

Emburey, aiming towards mid-wicket, was bowled by a full length ball from Hogg and though Old and Willis mustered 24 for the last wicket, the last three wickets, which somehow contributed 221 at Headingley, mustered only 28 yesterday.

The Scoreboard

England: First innings:

G. Boycott, c Marsh, b Alderman	13
J. M. Brearley, c Border, b Lillee	48
D. I. Gower, c Hogg, b Alderman	0
G. A. Gooch, c Marsh, b Bright	21
M. W. Gatting, c Alderman, b Lillee	21
P. Willey, b Bright	16
I. T. Botham, b Alderman	26
J. E. Emburey, b Alderman	3
C. M. Old, not out	11
R. G. D. Willis, c Marsh b Alderman	13
Extras (b 1, lb 5, w 1, nb 10)	17

Total 189

Bowling	O	M	R	W
Lillee	18	4	61	2
Alderman	23.1	8	42	5
Hogg	16	3	49	1
Bright	12	4	20	2

Fall of wickets: 1-29, 2-29, 3-60, 4-101.
5-126, 6-145, 7-161, 8-161, 9-165.

Australia: First innings:

		Bowling	O	M	R	W
G. M. Wood, not out	6	Willis	4	1	8	0
J. Dyson, b Old	1					
A. R. Border, c Taylor, b Old	2	Old	5	4	1	2
R. J. Bright, not out	0	Emburey	2	2	0	0
Extras (b 4, lb 2, nb 4)	10					

Total (2 wkts) 19

Fall of wickets: 1-5, 2-14

Umpires: H. D. Bird & D. C. Oslear.

Teams – Fourth Test
England: Boycott, Brearley, Gower,
Gooch, Gatting, Willey, Botham,
Emburey, Old, Willis, Taylor
Australia: Wood, Dyson, Border, Bright,
Hughes, Yallop, Kent, Marsh, Lillee,
Hogg, Alderman

1 AUGUST 1981

Australia Take Lead; and Brearley's Wicket

England, falling 69 behind on the first innings, finished the second eventful day of the Fourth Cornhill Test at Edgbaston still 20 runs behind. Brearley was already out in the second innings but it was a far better position than had seemed likely for most of the day.

Wood, Hughes and Kent had batted with greater application than the England batsmen had done, and perhaps on a rather more straightforward pitch, though that may have partly reflected the fact that much of the bowling was less accurate than Australia's on Thursday.

Willis contributed 28 no-balls, but happily Old was at his best and Emburey posed more and more problems as the day progressed.

The England fielding was not always immaculate but two straight throws by Old and Brearley earned two welcome run-outs. The first, which removed Wood, whose batting carried a greater look of permanence than anyone's, was probably the biggest single influence on an entertaining though sometimes petulant day's play.

71

It finished, however, with jovial exchanges between Lillee and a previously critical crowd whose lungs compared well with those of their counterparts in Sydney. By then Brearley, after playing Alderman twice off his legs for four, had been lbw to a ball from Lillee which came back at him rather low.

The remainder of England's 55 minutes' batting was safely negotiated by Boycott and Gower. Gower came down late on one or two balls which kept low and survived a loud appeal for a catch at the wicket off Hogg, but played some nicely-timed strokes between times.

It was one of those misty, overcast mornings when in theory the ball should swing a lot but does not. Old did pass Wood's bat once or twice early on but Wood played very straight and seldom looked in trouble throughout the morning.

IDEAL NIGHTWATCHMAN

Bright meanwhile played the ideal nightwatchman's innings, occupying the bowlers at their freshest for an hour and making 27 of the 43 scored before Botham brought a ball back to have him lbw.

Hughes began with a hook which was not far off square leg and survived an lbw appeal which must also have been close. But he was soon playing splendidly and by lunch, at 111 for three, Australia had by sensible batting won back the initiative after their uneasy start of Thursday evening.

Two overs after lunch England had a slice of luck. Wood played Emburey to mid-off and ran somewhat boldly. Old threw at the bowler's wicket and hit it just before Wood arrived.

There soon followed a weird over by the suddenly ferocious Willis who worked himself up to top pace and delivered a number of short balls to Hughes. The umpires conferred but, presumably because on this pitch even a chest-high bumper was a feat of Herculean strength and as likely to damage the bowler as the batsman, nothing happened.

Hughes responded by refusing singles to third man and long leg, partly no doubt because Australia were already doing nicely off no balls – three in the over – and partly because Yallop, who had been out at Headingley fending a short ball from Willis off his chest, had only just come in.

Anyhow on a pitch which had generally required a full length, with the odd variation, this did not bother Hughes and Yallop who made 41 in 45 minutes before Old moved a full-length ball in to have Hughes lbw.

The light was murky when Kent arrived to make an under-standably nervous-looking start to his first Test innings. It soon gave way to some of the best strokes of the match to date, fine, cleanly hit blows off front foot and back.

One of them took Australia into the lead and though Botham was swinging the ball a little now from the City End, the batsmen were not exactly pinned down either by him or Emburey.

15 minutes before tea, however, at 203, Yallop advanced down the pitch to Emburey and aimed to drive him to mid-on. The ball turned and bowled him.

In the third over after tea Marsh made room to hit a shortish ball from Emburey off the back foot and suffered a fate which had always seemed a possibility on this pitch. The ball was a faster one which kept low and bowled him.

There had been moments of ill-humour previously so that the stage was set for the arrival of Lillee, who is not exactly demure on such occasions. He was soon engaged in ostentatious exchanges with Gooch and Taylor and his presence prompted Willis to bowl an over which cost 15 runs.

This included half-volleys, long hops and three no-balls, of which one was unloosed with even the back foot over the front crease.

An end was mercifully put to an unattractive piece of cricket by Emburey who, with a subtlety not at first apparent, produced a half-volley outside the legs of the excellent Kent. It might well have gone for six but was hit almost straight to Willis at deep square leg.

In the same over Lillee went for a run to Brearley, at wide mid-on, but Brearley's quick throw to the striker's end hit the stumps and ran out Hogg before he had received a ball. In Emburey's next over Lillee, projecting a massive on-drive, was bowled.

The Scoreboard

England: First innings
189

Second innings:

		Bowling	O	M	R	W
G. Boycott, not out	9	Lillee	5	3	7	1
J. M. Brearley, lbw b Lillee	13	Alderman	6	1	23	0
D. I. Gower, not out	20	Hogg	2	0	12	0
Extras (lb 3, w 4)	7					

Total (1 wkt) 49

Fall of wickets 1-20.

73

FOURTH TEST   SECOND DAY

Australia: First innings

G. M. Wood, run out	38
J. H. Dyson, b Old	1
A. R. Border, c Taylor, b Old	2
R. J. Bright, lbw b Botham	27
K. J. Hughes, lbw b Old	47
G. N. Yallop, b Emburey	30
M. F. Kent, c Willis, b Emburey	46
R. W. Marsh, b Emburey	2
D. K. Lillee, b Emburey	18
R. M. Hogg, run out	0
T. M. Alderman, not out	3
Extras (b 4, lb 19, nb 21)	44

Total 258

Fall of wickets: 1-5, 2-14, 3-62, 4-115, 5-166, 6-203, 7-220, 8-253, 9-252.

Bowling	O	M	R	W
Willis	19	3	63	0
Old	21	8	44	3
Emburey	26.5	12	43	4
Botham	20	1	64	1

Umpires: H. D. Bird & D. O. Oslear.

3 AUGUST 1981

Botham's 5-1 Spell Puts England One Up in Series

It happened again yesterday, amid even more hysterical excitement than at Headingley, for there was a much bigger crowd. When all seemed lost, England snatched back the Fourth Cornhill Test at Edgbaston, bowled out Australia for 121, and won by 29 runs.

The margin was slightly larger than before, the final swing came much more suddenly, but the matchwinner was the same, Ian Botham, this time with the ball.

He took over when Australia, needing 151 to win, were 114 for five. Mike Brearley, the captain, said later that Botham came on with some diffidence because he thought others were bowling better. Anyhow, he took the last five wickets for one run in 28 balls.

At 10 minutes to four, Australia, with Kent and Marsh together and only 37 needed, were starting what looked like a final assault against bowlers who were entitled to be wilting a little on a hot, tense day.

Forty minutes and eight overs later, it was all over. Australia, who a fortnight ago seemed about to go two up in the series, were 2-1 down in it.

EMBUREY'S BATTING

There was another parallel with Headingley in that the 52 runs which John Emburey coaxed from the last two England wickets on Saturday evening, and at the end of an innings in which England had scarcely distinguished themselves, proved all-important. There is a huge difference between having to make 100 and having to make 150.

Of England's early batting on Saturday, all that needs, to be said at the moment of a glorious but very lucky victory is that in cutting out the rather light-hearted approach of the first innings, they went too far to the other extreme with a strokelessness which could only keep the bowlers on top.

In a way, yesterday's was a more remarkable win for the England bowlers than that at Headingly, for they had a slower, less bouncy pitch. Because it was so sluggish, the occasional eccentricity was less likely to be fatal, the error could often be corrected, the bat removed in time.

Yet in any close match like this on an unpredictable and, for Edgbaston, utterly untypical pitch, luck plays a big part. Yesterday England had some astonishing pieces of luck.

As they occurred, England seemed to be strengthened by the thought that they really could do it again, while Australia felt the shadow of Headingley draw ever nearer.

For much of the day, after Australia at 29 for three had made a bad start, it seemed as if they could recover. Allan Border batted for 3½ hours and Australia were at one time 87 for three and again 105 for four.

But every time Australia had victory within sight, a wicket fell and England were back again. Border's wicket was lost to the biggest slice of luck of all, when a ball from Emburey stood straight up as he played forward and gave him no chance.

The luck had turned against Australia early on a cloudless morning when Dyson and Border resumed at nine for one as if the task was not one to cause great difficulty if approached with reasonable care. There was nothing then to suggest that at lunch Border would have added only 11 runs and would then have batted 2½ hours in all for 13.

WILLIS'S RENEWED FIRE

After 20 minutes Willis, who as at Headingley found new fire and accuracy in the second innings, brought a ball back sharply to have Dyson lbw, so sharply that the batsman clearly thought it would have missed the leg stump.

After another 20 minutes Hughes hooked Willis slightly off-balance but with a fine ringing sound from the bat. The ball might have gone anywhere but flew straight to Emburey at deep backward square leg near the boundary and was safely taken.

Willis's next ball must have been within a whisker of bowling Yallop but a slow recovery was on the way. Apart from an awkward low chance which Border gave to Brearley at first slip off Willis when he was nine and the score 40, there were no further Australian mishaps before lunch when the pressure seemed to be easing on the batsmen.

Emburey turned the occasional ball but could not at first create the same apprehension in the batsmen as had Bright, left arm over the wicket and with the rough to aim at. Botham tried a spell well wide of the off stump but without encouraging the two left-handers to err or even to play very often.

After lunch Border and Yallop gathered confidence and when Willis, who had bowled his heart nearly out for 90 minutes before lunch, came on again, Yallop played him for two fours behind square leg.

In Emburey's next over, however, as the match was slipping away from England, Yallop nicked a ball on to his boot whence it popped up to Botham at silly point. Yallop and Border had added 58.

By now the bowlers had inevitably lost their freshness and Border, in his fourth hour, seemed to have worked out what was needed. But at 105 he could do nothing about the ball from Emburey which lobbed from high up the bat to short leg.

His departure made it certain that this would be a completed Test match without an individual 50, the first since the first Test between the West Indies and England in 1934-35 which was played on a wet pitch in Barbados.

MARSH YORKED

At 114 for five Australia still seemed to have matters under control, but after Marsh had hit Emburey off the back foot for four he pulled across a yorker in the second over of Botham's spell which was being bowled very accurately on a full length. The next ball came back rather low to have Bright lbw.

The removal of two seasoned, capable batsmen in two balls was a devastating blow for Australia. England by contrast had come a long and heartening way from the nadir of mid-afternoon on Saturday, when, with six wickets down, they were only 46 runs on.

Lillee stayed for 20 minutes amid a rare din for a Test match in England and then drove at a wide ball from Botham leaving him, Taylor dived a long way, and, having got there, was lucky to hold the catch at the second attempt.

Kent, looking reasonably authoritative amid the hubbub, began refusing singles to keep the strike from Hogg and had just spurned one when he drove across an inswinger from Botham and was bowled. It took Botham three balls to produce an inswinging yorker to bowl Alderman and, only 12 days after Headingley, history had repeated itself.

The Man of the Match award was given to Ian Botham and in the excitement of the final stages of another extraordinary England victory not many would have argued with the choice. But, on sober reflection, the bowling of John Emburey in each innings and the vital 37 runs which he made at the end of England's second innings were the contributions which made it all possible.

The Scoreboard

England: First innings
189

Second innings:

G. Boycott, c Marsh, b Bright	29	
J. M. Brearley, lbw, b Lillee	13	
D. I. Gower, c Border, b Bright	23	
G. A. Gooch, b Bright	21	
M. W. Gatting, b Bright	39	
P. Willey, b Bright	5	
I. T. Botham, c Marsh, b Lillee	3	
C. Old, c Marsh, b Alderman	23	
J. E. Emburey, not out	37	
R. W. Taylor, lbw, b Alderman	8	
R. G. D. Willis, c Marsh, b Alderman	2	
Extras (lb 6, w 1, nb 9)	16	

Total 219

Fall of wickets: 1-16, 2-52, 3-89, 4-98, 5-110, 6-116, 7-154, 8-167, 9-217.

Australia: First innings
258

Second innings:

J. Dyson, lbw, b Willis	13
G. M. Wood, lbw, b Old	2
A. R. Border, c Gatting, b Emburey	40
K. J. Hughes, c Emburey, b Willis	5
G. N. Yallop, c Botham, b Emburey	30
M. F. Kent, b Botham	10
R. W. Marsh, b Botham	4
R. J. Bright, lbw, b Botham	0
D. K. Lillee, c Taylor, b Botham	3
R. M. Hogg, not out	0
T. M. Alderman, b Botham	0
Extras (b 1, lb 2, nb 11)	14

Total 121.

Fall of wickets: 1-2, 2-19, 3-29, 4-87, 5-105, 6-114, 8-120, 9-121.

Bowling	O	M	R	W
Lillee	26	9	51	2
Alderman	22	5	65	3
Hogg	10	3	19	0
Bright	34	17	68	5

Bowling	O	M	R	W
Willis	20	6	37	2
Old	11	4	19	1
Emburey	22	10	40	2
Botham	14	9	11	5

England won by 29 runs

Gooch and Willey in Danger

One useful by-product of England's victory at Edgbaston with a day to spare was that it gave the selectors an extra chance to look at first-class matches elsewhere.

In recent weeks there has often been none played between the end of one Test and the picking of the team for the next.

But for what, or whom, are they now looking? Sunday's result means a major reconstruction will probably be delayed until the team for India is chosen, unless by some happy chance the series were decided at Old Trafford, allowing a freer hand for the Oval.

If the Edgbaston Test had been lost, one could have foreseen various chances such as the strengthening of the later batting by the recall of Knott, now making runs again. But Taylor played a vital part in helping Emburey to raise the precious extra runs at the end of the second innings.

Gooch's batting when the ball moves about has caused concern and the position of Willey must have come under review.

BATTING OPTIONS

He has made two fine aggressive hundreds against the West Indies' fast bowlers, but if he is going to be coming in against spin, as at Edgbaston, and if he is not required to bowl, a chance might be given to another batsman such as Tavare, Parker or Randall.

Excluding Botham, the contributions of the five batsmen who have played eight completed innings in the series are led by those of the two youngest, Gower (226 runs) and Gatting (218). Behind them are Boycott (208), Willey (179) and Gooch (124).

In defence of all of them, it can be said that, in three Tests anyhow, they have batted on pitches on which no one was ever really in. The unpredictable was always just around the corner.

Though it seemed unlikely in April that the two veteran former invalids, Willis and Old, would be carrying the burden of England's fast bowling in August, here they are.

NO PENSION YET

Willis bowled with the same fire on the bounceless pitch at Edgbaston as he had at Headingley where only a fortnight ago today he took his eight for 43.

This is scarcely the moment to pension him off – or for that matter Old who, for much of the last Test, was England's best bowler and whose wickets were those of Australia's first four batsmen, Wood, Dyson, Border and Hughes.

The opportunity may well be taken to include a younger player in the 12, if only for experience, depending on what the selectors see in the meantime. Allott might well be a suitable choice for Old Trafford. Les Taylor and Parsons will have been watched at Leicester, as well as Parker and Mendis.

The selectors' main trouble in the past year has been that there have been no obvious alternatives, especially bowlers, of Test calibre forcing themselves to be picked by their consistency.

ILL-BALANCED PROGRAMME

They have also been handicapped by the cock-eyed arrangement of tours. If one excludes the Jubilee Test in Bombay in February 1980 which they won easily. England have played their last 17 Tests against the West Indies, or Australia, their toughest opponents.

Nobody asks for the other extreme – a long sequence of relatively easy matches against weaker opponents who are often playing in conditions strange to them.

But a middle course which gives the selectors a chance to bring in new players when they are not under the same hypercritical scrutiny which exists in a Test series in England would ease the transition. India this winter provides such an opportunity.

---

5 AUGUST 1981

Botham – 1910 Edition

S everal readers have kindly written pointing out the similarity between "Botham's Test" at Headingley and "Fowler's Match" – Eton v Harrow at Lord's in 1910.

One of them was present on that distant occasion and testifies to the agony of watching. Others have asked for their memories to be refreshed, which shall be done forthwith.

Harrow made 232 on a soft, turning pitch and when bad light ended play early on the first evening had taken five Eton wickets for 40.

Next day Eton were out for 67. They followed on and soon after lunch were 65 for five, still 100 behind. It was at this point that Fowler, the Eton captain, who had been top scorer in the first innings, made a vigorous counter-attack, worth 64 runs. But when the ninth wicket fell, his side were only four runs ahead.

50 FOR LAST WICKET

K. A. Lister-Kaye, described as a rustic batsman with a good eye, and J. N. Manners, a rackets player said to be at his best in a crisis, then sailed into the Harrow bowling and made 50 for the last wicket in 23 minutes. Harrow therefore needed 55 to win in the last innings.

Fowler was described by the late H.S. Altham as "a slowish bowler, accurate, of skilful varying pace and sharp off-spin." He bowled one of Harrow's openers first ball and soon was working his way through the rest of the batting.

In the Harrow side were several players well-known later in first-class cricket, such as T. O. Jameson, and G. F. Earle. There was a pause while Jameson, who had opened the innings but did not score for 50 minutes, recovered from a painful blow. Fowler eventually bowled him, thus taking his eighth wicket, and Harrow were 32 for nine.

Now Harrow's last pair. O. B. Graham and the future Field Marshal Earl Alexander, of Tunis, stood firm amid the hubbub and excitement of the packed ground of those days. Thirteen runs were added and then a leg-break from A. J. Steel had Alexander caught in the slips.

Fowler had taken eight for 23 in 10 overs, Eton had won by nine runs, and a heavy defeat had been turned into victory much as it was to be at Headingley 71 years later.

After that cruel disappointment of 1910 the losers did not beat Eton for a further 29 years.

Captain Robert St. Leger Fowler, M.C., joined the army on leaving Eton and was awarded the Sword of Honour at Sandhurst. His cricket was restricted by his career as a soldier but he played twice for Hampshire in 1924. He died in 1925 aged 34.

Fifth Test

OLD TRAFFORD

13-17 AUGUST 1981

Three Changes – and Questions Against Each

Eengland make three changes for Thursday's Fifth Cornhill Test match at Old Trafford, bringing in Tavare, Knott and Underwood, as it happens all of Kent, for Willey, Taylor and Dilley, who incidentally aggravated his shoulder injury again on Saturday.

These changes are clearly a temporary move, probably bearing little relation to the selection of the team for next winter's tour of India – or even for the last Test at the Oval if England by then are leading 3-1.

They are designed to win this coming match which, of course, is a very proper approach. All one hopes is that the judgments on which they seem to be based are sound.

It is foreseen that the pitch at Old Trafford will take spin. The one on which Lancashire played Worcestershire last weekend took so much that the side batting second apparently had no chance.

That pitch may have been an exception because it had been used for a one-day match previously and had had an unusual preparation. But the selectors seem to have satisfied themselves that before the end of a five-day match the ball may well be turning.

WELCOME VARIETY

So back comes Underwood who ironically was dropped for last year's Old Trafford Test. Knott was dropped two matches later.

The return of Underwood provides welcome variety but has led to an attempt to strengthen the later batting. Hence the return of Knott, who mustered only 36 runs in seven Test innings last year but, one likes to think, is batting better again this season.

The selectors seem to have had mixed luck when they watched them recently and the fear is that Knott and Underwood have been picked for what they once were, rather than for what they are at present. Yet for the purposes of this particular exercise, it may well work.

Tavare's method may not appear in any coaching manual, especially the grip with hands wide apart, but with his studious application and consistency he has been rather unlucky not to have been called on earlier in a period when England have been short of an effective batsman at No. 3.

BOGGED DOWN

The spectre of his becoming bogged down, as at Lord's last year, and perhaps in company with Boycott and Brearley, probably haunted the selectorial corridors.

Of those left out, Willey, as suggested in these columns last week, ceased to be so important if he was not needed to bowl and if the opposition bowling was no longer based on the extreme pace which he plays so stoutly.

Taylor was not quite at his best at Edgbaston but his undemonstrative neatness still makes most other modern wicketkeepers look clumsy.

Most of these changes were predictable in the circumstances and the selectors' most difficult decision may be whom to leave out of the 12, for they have picked only five front-line bowlers including Botham.

Either they leave out a fast bowler, presumably Old, whose steadiness was of great value in both recent victories, and rely on Gooch if needed. Or they leave out a batsman. But which? A case can be made out for each of them and, because of strokelessness or impetuousness, against each.

Four bowlers were enough at Edgbaston but there is nothing like putting all your faith in four to make one of them break down. The final choice may well depend rather more than usual on the prevailing conditions.

Two days before the Fifth Test started Old had to withdraw through injury and was replaced by Paul Allott of Lancashire who was to play in his first Test match.

13 AUGUST 1981

Australia Call Whitney from County Match

Australia took the unprecedented step of calling a player out of a County Championship match after it had started yesterday and Mike Whitney, 22, a left-arm fast-medium bowler from New South Wales, will play in the Fifth Cornhill Test against England at Old Trafford today.

He has been in England for this summer playing for Fleet-wood in the Northern League, and has been registered for Gloucestershire, for whom he took two for nine in his eight overs in the John Player match against Surrey last Sunday.

He was due to play in his seventh first-class match against Hampshire at Cheltenham yesterday when Gloucestershire reported to Lord's that they had received an inquiry from the Australian management about Whitney's possible availability for Old Trafford.

There is a Schweppes Championship playing condition which allows a player to be withdrawn after a match has started if he is required for a Test match by England, but not if he is required by another country.

This distinction, however, was waived yesterday by the TCCB. "In the circumstances we thought it would be right and proper if the same rule applied to Australia," said Donald Carr, the TCCB secretary, yesterday.

HAMPSHIRE AGREEMENT

The call for Whitney came through after the match had started, though Gloucestershire were batting and he had not taken the field. Their opponents, Hampshire, had agreed in advance to a substitution if necessary and Whitney set off for the North.

He is needed because Lawson's back injury has not healed and Hogg could not guarantee that his back would stand up to a five-day Test. Carl Rackemann, of Queensland, who has been playing for Surrey Second XI, has been in reserve throughout the tour but he, too, is not fully fit.

Whitney, an apprentice maintenance engineer with Qantas, made a promising start for New South Wales last season and would have played more often but for a surfing accident.

"I can't believe this is all happening," he said yesterday. He comes into the Australian side in the happy position of having nothing to lose. Australia have become 2-1 down in the series in the most galling way, beaten successively by 18 and 29 runs, and the injuries to Lawson and Hogg have weakened them where they seemed earlier in the series to have a clear advantage.

PITCH STILL SOFT

However, they announced their team last night with Whitney for Hogg the only change and they have a great record for bouncing back not when they have been written off, which seldom happens, but when they think they have been written off.

England's choice from 12 was not eased by finding a pitch which was still soft after a record 24-hour rainfall a week ago and which has had insufficient sun since to dry it out. Manchester escaped the unrelieved sunshine of other parts yesterday.

In view of the shakiness of England's batting in the series, admittedly largely on unpredictable pitches, it would make sense, except on a supremely easy batting pitch, to play all the batsmen and rely on four bowlers plus Gooch.

This would mean leaving out Allott for this match and no doubt launching him at the Oval.

However, there will doubtless be much earnest discussion on the pitch and likely weather conditions this morning, augmented by the views of Mike Brearley whose arrival was delayed until yesterday evening by a slightly sore throat.

The omens are favourable especially if the ball turns, but two wins by 18 runs and 29 runs and all that went before them scarcely promote boundless confidence.

● Alec Bedser, the chairman of selectors, said last night. "We didn't know the pitch had been flooded and what effect the storms have had on it, we just don't know. It's certainly not in the condition we expected."

14 AUGUST 1981

Same Old Story for England – Except Tavare

Anyone who watched the ball moving about on a grey day and England struggling to reach 175 for nine off 74 overs at Old Trafford yesterday could have been excused for thinking that he had seen it all before.

There was the same contrast in the batting between the sober fallibility of the seniors and the sparkle provided by Gower and especially Gatting prior to an ill-chosen and fatal stroke.

There was Alderman bowling away splendidly at one end
and taking four more wickets to help him past Lillee's Australian record of 31 for a series in England.

The difference this time was that Tavare dug in at one end for
all but half-an-hour of the 5¼ hours' play possible and at last
provided the discipline and application which has been missing
at No. 3.

He was out in the last over, caught at slip while slashing at a
ball leaving him, but had made the first 50 by an England No. 3
in 22 innings and the highest score by one since Brian Rose
made 70 on this ground 13 months and 12 Test matches ago.

LIMITED RANGE

Tavare played very straight, with a limited range but with
scarcely a false stroke until he opened up after the fall of the
eighth wicket at 137. He then made 29 of the 38 useful runs
added to an undistinguished England innings.

There were certainly excuses in the pitch, the damp weather
and the rest given the Australian bowlers by an 85 minute break
for rain over lunch but overall it was an inglorious and
inadequate performance which one would expect a strong
Australian batting side, perhaps this one, to leave well behind.

Tavare's wicket was the second taken by Michael Whitney,
the young bowler plucked from obscurity for this match. He
was lucky to have helpful conditions, helpful batting and two
high-class bowlers in Lillee and Alderman to assist him but he
bowled with life and accuracy and weathered his extraordinary
elevation remarkably well.

LATE RE-THINKING

The final choice of England's team reflected some re-thinking
born of conditions which were not what were expected when
the 12 were chosen. Underwood's return in place of Willey had
led to the recall of Knott instead of the luckless Taylor, in order
to lengthen the batting.

Yet, in the event, Underwood was left out. Moreover, the
Edgbaston experiment of dropping Gooch down the order was
not pursued and he came out with Boycott when England chose
to bat on a pitch not certain to improve with age, even though it
carried enough grass to allow the ball to move a lot yesterday.

The first matter to be attended to was the passing by Boycott
of Colin Cowdrey's 7,624, the previous highest aggregate in

Test cricket by an English batsman: the seven runs needed were completed with a well-timed stroke off Alderman to the square leg boundary but, two balls later Boycott nicked one off the inside edge on to his thigh.

He was unlucky that it lobbed just far enough for Marsh – diving forward – to take a good catch. In the next over, Gooch met a ball from Lillee which came back a long way, apparently just low enough to have him lbw.

In the third-wicket stand of 32 which followed, Tavare, playing very straight and not playing at all unless it was necessary, looked safe enough. Gower's activities against the moving ball were harder on English nerves.

Before he had scored, he aimed to pull a ball from Alderman, edged it on to some part of his body and was lucky that Wood – running back from first slip – could not quite reach it.

After 75 minutes, Whitney, until Tuesday a stranger to some of the Australian side, had his first bowl in what is only his seventh first-class match. He bowled one ball and it rained. In some parts of the world, he would command a huge fee for producing such results.

Whitney, left-arm fast-medium, is of medium height and broad build in the mould of Gary Gilmour, perhaps rather faster in pace. He bowled a good length and, when they resumed after lunch, had Gower missed at first slip. Wood, presumably slow to sight the ball, was hit in the face and retired for repairs and a precautionary X-ray.

Whitney had only to wait until his fourth over before Gower, who among less impressive strokes, had driven Alderman on the off side several times, played him loosely into gully's midriff. In the next over, Brearley was lbw to Alderman, much as Gooch had been to Lillee.

Gatting was looking busily for runs from the start, Tavare played soundly at the other end and gradually the runs began to flow until they were coming in a gush, 47 in 55 minutes. Then Gatting, having played very well, fell from grace as he did after another otherwise admirable innings at Edgbaston.

This time he was hooking. He is a keen and usually sensible hooker and Lillee's first two short balls to him were put away with gusto. Lillee thereupon produced an even shorter ball which arrived as Gatting was almost finishing the stroke and popped up to slip off the glove.

Botham steered the next ball downwards into the gully where Bright dived and took a brilliant left-handed catch near

87

the ground. This was 109 for six.

The light had never been good since the rain and became worse after tea but Tavare went on impassively. Knott stayed with him for an hour but, soon after surviving a stumping chance off Bright, was caught at second slip off a modest stroke.

This was soon emulated by Emburey, also off Alderman, with the difference that this time Border fractured a finger, though it will not apparently stop him from batting.

Australia then had two substitutes on, for Yallop was off with a migraine, and one of these, Chappell, had to be replaced when he also damaged a finger in trying to catch Tavare at third man.

By then the 18,000 crowd was being greatly cheered not only by Tavare's increased activity but by the stout support given him by the new local hero, Allott, in his first Test match.

Tavare was 40 when Allott came in and was then given a widespread defensive field which invited the single and also put off the chance of Australia having to bat in a poor light after some hours in the field.

The 38 runs conceded in an hour would be considered cheap ordinarily. In this series, one wonders.

The Scoreboard

England: First innings

G. A. Gooch, lbw, b Lillee	10
G. Boycott, c Marsh, b Aldermann	10
C. J. Tavare, c Alderman, b Whitney	69
D. I. Gower, c Yallop, b Whitney	23
J. M. Brearley, lbw, b Alderman	2
M. W. Gatting, c Border, b Lillee	32
I. T. Botham, c Bright, b Lillee	0
A. P. E. Knott, c Border, b Alderman	13
J. E. Emburey, c Border, b Alderman	1
P. J. W. Allott, not out	9
R. G. D. Willis, not out	0
Extras (lb 5, w 1)	6

Total (9 wkts) 175

Fall of wickets: 1-19, 2-25, 3-57, 4-62, 5-109, 6-109, 7-131, 8-137, 9-175.

Bowling	O	M	R	W
Lillee	18	7	40	3
Alderman	27	5	68	4
Whitney	13	3	31	2
Bright	16	6	30	0

Umpires: D. J. Constant & K. E. Palmer.

Teams – Fifth Test

England: Gooch, Boycott, Tavare, Gower, Brearley, Gatting, Botham, Knott, Emburey, Allott, Willis

Australia: Wood, Kent, Hughes, Yallop, Dyson, Border, Marsh, Bright, Alderman, Lillee, Whitney

Australia Crash again as England Seize Control

No one could have dreamed when England began the second day of the Fifth Cornhill Test at 175 for nine yesterday that 20 minutes before tea they would be batting again with a lead of 101. Yet it happened – and by the end Boycott and Tavare had extended the lead to 171 with only Gooch out.

A last-wicket stand of 56 by Allott and Willis – Allott's 52 not out came in his first Test innings – gave the match a push towards England whose last two wickets made 96.

Willis's capture of Australia's first three wickets in his third over added a mighty shove.

In all, Australia lost their first four wickets in seven balls, subsiding from 20 for no wicket to 24 for four, and though there was a partial recovery from 59 for six led by Kent, they were bowled out for 130.

Their extraordinary innings lasted only $2\frac{1}{2}$ hours and 30.2 overs which is Australia's shortest since 1902. Yet it contained 16 fours and a six.

RELIABLE HEIGHT

The ball still moved a little but usually at a reliable height. England held almost all their catches, including a marvellous one by Gower, but will doubtless bowl better on other days for only a fraction of their success yesterday.

It is a fair guess that the batsmen of both sides have lost confidence through three awkward pitches earlier in the series. Whatever the reason, there has been nothing in the conditions at Old Trafford to warrant the loss of 20 wickets for 361 runs.

But let nothing detract from another inspired piece of bowling by Bob Willis, who in one over struck the really devastating blows; from the heartening first appearance with bat and ball of Paul Allott, and from the contribution of the inevitable Ian Botham, who took three wickets and three catches.

ALLOTT'S FIFTY

This eventful day began with 50 minutes of rich entertainment in which Allott and Willis made 56 for the last wicket. Allott is to the back foot what his predecessor, Dilley, is to the

89

front foot, and for some reason he was accommodated with a lot that was short, especially by Whitney and then by Alderman.

Favouring the area square on the off-side, Allott raced past his previous highest first-class score of 30, batting as if the whole thing was simple.

When the new ball was taken by Alderman, he finished an over costing 16 runs by hitting the last three balls for four with roughly the same stroke. The first went where intended past cover point, the next two off the inside edge past the wicket-keeper.

Willis, who had supported him with increasing confidence, skied Lillee's next ball to deep mid-off and the fun was over, leaving Allott unconquered and the sobering fear that this would only have been possible if the pitch had lost its modest eccentricity of Thursday.

This view was endorsed a few minutes later when Wood, with great assurance, hooked the last two balls of Willis' first over for four and six, and followed with another hook for four in his second over.

Whatever the pitch might do by the fifth day, it looked as if it was not going to be of much help to the bowlers in the meantime, especially as the sun was now coming out after another morning of cloud and drizzle.

Then in 10 minutes everything changed. Dyson playing a short ball down in Willis's third over was not quite on top of it and was caught at third slip by Botham.

BOTHAM'S DIVE

That was the first ball of the over. Hughes hit the third, a wide long hop, high on the offside for four but was lbw when the fourth came back to him off a full length.

Yallop edged the sixth to third slip where Botham dived to take one-handed a fine catch which needed the umpire's confirmation that it had carried. Wood, playing across Allott's next ball, was lbw.

There was nearly another even stranger incident, in Willis's next over when, before Kent had scored, a short ball momentarily lodged on his person whence it dropped and, as he tried to kick it away, rolled up against the stumps.

Otherwise the remaining half-hour before lunch passed uneventfully with a generous supply of long hops which Kent and Border dealt with efficiently until the last over.

For his fourth ball of this, Botham went round the wicket to Border and bowled a half-volley wide outside the off stump which Border drove off the middle of the bat.

The ball was flying like a bullet over fourth slip when Gower caught it magnificently right-handed above his head. So lunch was taken with the improbable score, after only 11.4 overs, of 58 for 5.

Botham finished his over after lunch, Marsh taking a run off his first ball. But off the first ball of Willis's next over Marsh, deciding too late not to play, gave Botham a straightforward catch at third slip.

Kent, upstanding striker of the ball that he is, was now playing with such panache that he prompted Brearley to set a singular field of three slips and six men round the boundary. All went well for Australia, and especially for Kent, until he had made 52 handsomely out of 79 in 69 minutes.

At this point Emburey was brought on and, having conceded four runs off his first ball, which was short, had Kent caught at the wicket trying to force off the back foot the third ball which was not so short. Kent and Bright had added 45.

Again the innings proceeded for a while without promising much to the bowlers. Willis at last came off, after bowling throughout from the Stretford End, and was replaced by Botham, whose first ball was a half volley going down the leg side. Lillee turned it straight into Gooch's hands at backward square leg.

BAFFLING EPISODE

Whitney was soon yorked by Allott. When Botham had one of the more obdurate batsmen, Bright, caught at the wicket, the 21,000 crowd, on whom the gates had been closed early on, had seen the end of one of the more baffling episodes in the history of England – Australia Test matches.

They then saw Gooch bowled behind his legs, playing across a ball in Alderman's second over. In 10 innings in the series Gooch has made only 139 runs, nearly half of them in the drawn Second Test at Lord's where the ball moved about less than on the four other grounds.

At this point there was clearly an urgent need to bring some permanence back to the business of batting, to play straight and to do nothing to allow Australia a spark of hope.

In Boycott and Tavare England had the right batsmen for the task.

The Scoreboard

England: First innings

G. A. Gooch, lbw, b Lillee	10
G. Boycott, c Marsh, b Alderman	10
C. J. Tavare, c Alderman, b Whitney	69
D. I. Gower, c Yallop, b Whitney	23
J. M. Brearley, lbw, b Alderman	2
M. W. Gatting, c Border, b Lillee	32
I. T. Botham, c Bright, b Lillee	0
A. P. E. Knott, c Border, b Alderman	13
J. E. Emburey, c Border, b Alderman	1
P. J. W. Allott, not out	52
R. G. J. Willis, c Hughes, b Lillee	11
Extras (lb 6, w 2)	8

Total 231

Fall of wickets: 1-19, 2-25, 3-57, 4-62,
5-109, 6-109, 7-131, 8-137, 9-175.

Bowling	O	M	R	W
Lillee	24.1	8	55	4
Alderman	29	5	88	4
Whitney	17	3	50	2
Bright	16	6	30	0

Second innings

G. A. Gooch, b Alderman	5
G. Boycott not out	31
C. J. Tavare, not out	29
Extras (b 1, lb 3, nb 1)	5

Total (1 wkt) 70

Fall of wicket: 1-7.

Bowling	O	M	R	W
Lillee	11	5	23	0
Alderman	13	5	23	1
Whitney	9	1	19	0
Bright	3	3	0	0

Australia: First innings

G. M. Wood, lbw, b Allott	19
J. Dyson, c Botham, b Willis	0
K. J. Hughes, lbw, b Willis	4
G. N. Yallop, c Botham, b Willis	0
M. F. Kent, c Knott, b Emburey	52
A. R. Border, c Gower b Botham	11
R. W. Marsh, c Botham, b Willis	1
R. J. Bright, c Knott, b Botham	22
D. K. Lillee, c Gooch, b Botham	13
M. J. Whitney, b Allott	0
T. M. Alderman, not out	2
Extras (nb 6)	6

Total 130

Fall of wickets: 1-20, 2-24, 3-24, 4-24,
5-58, 6-59, 7-104, 8-125, 9-126.

Bowling	O	M	R	W
Willis	14	0	63	4
Allott	6	1	17	2
Botham	6.2	1	28	3
Emburey	4	0	16	1

Umpires: D. J. Constant & K. E. Palmer

England Poised to Win despite Yallop's Century

The full value of Ian Botham's batting on Saturday, and indeed that of Chris Tavare and the later batsmen, was made clear at Old Trafford yesterday.

Australia set off after lunch needing 506 to win in just over 10 hours. England took five of their wickets for 210 and, all being well, will win the match and the series to retain the Ashes today.

Yet England were lucky in the way they took several wickets, and the conditions are such that a target of around 350 might well have been within Australia's powers.

Graham Yallop played a high-class innings of 114 in under three hours, and his stand with another left-hander, Allan Border, was swinging along so confidently 40 minutes before the end, despite Border's broken finger, that anything seemed possible.

Australia needed exactly 100 more than any side has ever made in the last innings to win a Test match but so much had happened this summer which would be unthinkable in another series, that a momentous comeback was conceivable.

SLOW AND USELESS

There is always a danger when a pitch starts damp, as this did, that under sun it will eventually become slow and useless to fast bowlers.

The bowlers will tire and, when there are only four and include only one spinner, as in England's case, good batsmen may take full charge.

As it happened Australia cast away two valuable early wickets but there were long periods later when the bowlers were making little impression.

In the last hour, too, there were signs that Emburey might still pose problems at the end which some had thought would in time take spin.

Brearley let the England innings run on until lunch, which it did without much distinction, though it passed 400 for the first time in 21 Tests – none too soon in view of the ease with which the pitch was playing when the innings ended.

Saturday was a day of almost certainly unique batting contrasts. Yet Botham's magnificent 118 in 123 minutes, an exhibition which for clean hitting and spectacular strokes even out-did his 149 not out at Headingley, was largely dependent on

Chris Tavare's long painstaking defence.

SIX-HIT RECORD

Botham's hundred in 86 balls, one fewer than at Headingley, broke England v Australia Test records in one direction. It was the second fastest hundred, after Jessop's in 1902, and the six sixes (sprinkled among 13 fours) were the most ever hit in an innings.

At the other extreme Tavare's 50 in 306 minutes was one of the slowest recorded in English first-class cricket.

Yet it is highly improbable that Botham's innings could have been played without Tavare's. On Saturday morning it was clear that if Lillee and Alderman could be worn down – and they bowled splendidly on a pitch still giving them some help – the road beyond should be clear.

PAINFULLY SLOW

Four wickets were lost in the painfully slow adding of 34 runs, but not Tavare's. He has an imperturbable temperament and he has worked out exactly what he can and cannot do in his individual, very straight method.

He did his unglamorous job with such devotion and self-discipline that in a match in which he batted for nearly 12 hours, I cannot remember his giving a chance, except on the two occasions when he was out.

By the time Botham came in, having been out first ball in the first innings, Lillee and Alderman had already bowled 15 and 16 overs respectively.

He reconnoitred for a time, then played two strokes against Bright which impressed on Hughes the need for Alderman and Lillee, however jaded, to take the new ball when available.

ONSLAUGHT STARTS

Then it started. Lillee's first over cost 22 runs, including two hooks for six, one of which the capless Botham, unlike ordinary mortals, achieved with eye well off the ball.

In 4.2 overs there were 52 runs (Botham 47); in eight overs before tea, 76 (Botham 65). He went from 28 to 100 in 37 minutes and made his last 90 out of 103 in 13½ overs and 55 minutes.

In this historic display of immensely hard but controlled hitting he gave only two half-chances of running catches in the outfield. After Botham, Knott's revived batting carried on the good work.

Emburey pushed the tired bowling about so well that they had already made 63 in an hour for the eighth wicket when they resumed yesterday on the first sunny morning of the match before another packed crowd.

After 20 minutes, Knott, cutting at a wide short ball from Lillee, was out to one of the best catches of its type that those present will have seen for years.

Dyson, 60 yards from the bat at third man, ran hard to his right and hurled himself forward to hold the ball near the ground right-handed.

DYSON RUN OUT

I doubt if England ever viewed the task ahead in the last innings as a formality, but the prospect became slightly less forbidding when in Willis's second over Dyson played short and to the right of Gower, at cover-point and started for the reasonable run.

Wood started too and they were not far off crossing when Wood sent Dyson back. Gower threw accurately on the turn to Gatting at the stumps and Dyson was out by five yards.

This was a big help and so was the catch which Knott took low down the leg side when Wood mis-hooked a long hop from Allott outside the leg-stump in the sixth over.

The stand of 95 in 90 minutes between Hughes and Yallop which followed, and the ease with which Yallop especially batted, put matters in a proper perspective.

The attacking field was relaxed and Emburey came on, but it was Botham who brought a ball back to have Hughes lbw at 119.

Early in the fourth wicket stand of 79 between Yallop and Border two spectators sauntered on to the field, watched with interest by the police and made off with the bails from one wicket.

POLICE CHASE

They returned into the crowd rather more quickly than they had come with the constabulary in lively and ultimately fruitful pursuit.

That was the last light relief England had for some time. Yallop quietened down and, when 89, survived a hard chance .
off Allott to Tavare diving right at first-slip.

Yallop then began playing with great panache again. He reached a hundred in 2¾ hours off 116 balls by hooking Botham for four and he drove Allott straight for two more fours.

He was making it look supremely easy, when Emburey replaced Allott and, as his first ball, floated a full pitch away down the leg side, Yallop pulled across it, missed and it turned enough, presumably from some rough, to bowl him round his legs.

For 25 minutes Willis, bowling at his fastest, and Emburey gave Border and Kent a difficult time, Border clearly suffering much discomfort from his broken finger.

Then Emburey brought Kent forward and Brearley, very close at silly mid-off, caught him.

The Scoreboard

England: First innings
231
Second innings:

G. A. Gooch, b Alderman	5
G. Boycott, lbw, b Alderman	37
C. J. Tavare, c Kent, b Alderman	78
D. I. Gower, c Bright, b Lillee	1
M. W. Gatting, lbw, b Alderman	11
J. M. Brearley, c Marsh, b Alderman	3
I. T. Botham, c Marsh, b Whitney	118
A. P. E. Knott, c Dyson, b Lillee	59
J. E. Emburey, c Kent, b Whitney	57
P. J. W. Allott, c Hughes, b Bright	14
R. G. D. Willis, not out	5
Extras (b 1, lb 12, nb 3)	16
Total	404

Fall of wickets: 1-7, 2-79, 3-80, 4-98, 5-104, 6-253, 7-282, 8-346, 9-399.

Bowling	O	M	R	W
Lillee	46	13	137	2
Alderman	52	19	109	5
Whitney	27	6	74	2
Bright	26.4	11	68	1

Australia: First innings
130
Second innings:

G. M. Wood, c Knott, b Allott	6
J. Dyson, run out	5
K. J. Hughes, lbw, b Botham	43
G. N. Yallop, b Emburey	114
A. R. Border, not out	28
M. F. Kent, c Brearley, b Emburey	2
R. W. Marsh, not out	2
Extras (lb 1, w 1, nb 8)	10
Total (5 wkts)	210

Fall of wickets: 1-7, 2-24, 3-119, 4-198, 5-206.

Bowling	O	M	R	W
Willis	16	2	50	0
Allott	10	2	52	1
Botham	17	6	55	1
Emburey	17	3	43	2

Umpires: D. J. Constant & K. E. Palmer.

England Wait for Clincher

Engand won the Fifth Cornhill Test at Old Trafford by 103 runs, the rubber by three matches to one and retained the Ashes, but they needed four hours 35 minutes yesterday to take the last five Australian wickets.

And there were long periods in the freakish situation when an Australian win seemed a genuine possibility. Allan Border held one end throughout, undefeated after batting for nearly seven hours with the broken finger which he described as "more annoying than paining."

Marsh and Lillee played so comfortably with him on this mild true pitch that England, with only four bowlers, were sorely tried.

Even at the end the No. 11 batsman held out for 40 minutes, and it was not inconceivable that he might stay while Border and Australia earned an honourable draw.

Eventually the last man was prised out with 85 minutes to spare, Australia were out for 402, and a series, which has seldom followed a predictable pattern, was decided.

For the first 100 minutes the sixth-wicket stand of the left-handers Border and Marsh continued serenely from the overnight 210 towards the record 506 needed. After 40 minutes the valiant Border was hit on the bad hand (the left) and had to call for a pain-killing spray.

MARSH DROPPED

Otherwise he cut, drove and hooked as if in the best of health and form, and Marsh too only had one bad moment. He pulled Emburey high to the square-leg boundary where Gower, probably put off by finding himself almost over the rope as he shaped to take the catch, dropped it.

Emburey had looked the most likely bowler to take a wicket, but Willis, when he came on to take the new ball, was faster and more accurate than at the start, and in his second over, at 296, Marsh, driving, touched the ball to Knott.

After lunch Willis continued to drag some bounce out of the reluctant pitch and after 20 minutes dug in a ball which slanted awkwardly into Bright's body and was glanced down the leg side where Knott dived to take a fine catch.

Lillee looked more comfortable and before long was hooking and driving Botham in an over which cost 11 runs. In the last three hours, 149 were needed.

Hereabouts, Border began shielding Lillee from the faster bowling, tactics which, considering how well Lillee was playing, were hard to follow. But after a lot of singles had been refused Lillee was allowed to play an over from Allott.

At this point, 15 minutes before tea, England had toiled 85 minutes without a wicket, and only 133 were needed. Relief was at hand, for Lillee cut at a ball rather too near his body, hitting it hard but uppishly, and Botham jumped high to his right at second-slip to hold a marvellous two-handed catch.

BOTHAM STRIKES

Botham was brought on three overs later to deal with Alderman, whom he had lbw fourth ball. The tea interval was thus delayed for half-an-hour but Whitney, usually allowed only two balls an over by Border, played through this with growing confidence against Botham and Emburey.

When the interval was eventually taken, the situation was complicated by a bomb scare which led to two stands being cleared and the bigger scoreboard ceasing to function.

In the first over afterwards Border made a rare mistake against Emburey when trying to manipulate the strike and was dropped by Knott. It did not matter.

Willis was produced for Whitney in the next over, and his fifth ball was nicked on to the pad. Gatting fell forward at short-leg to catch it right-handed.

So only 28 days after England, needing 92 to avoid an innings defeat at Headingley with only three wickets left, were, as it seemed, within minutes of going 2-0 down in the series, they have won it 3-1.

Before the tour began, it looked as if they might just win if Botham recovered his bowling and if the ageing fast bowlers, the heroes of 1978-79, could be wound up for one last effort.

ONE-DAY SUCCESSES

This seemed less likely when Australia arrived with two splendid young bowlers in Alderman and Lawson and won the Prudential series, the First Test, had the better of the Second and the first three-and-a-half days of the Third.

What went wrong? Or to be more partisan, what went right?

The most obvious factor was that Botham became a great force again with his two brilliant hundreds and his five wickets for one run at Edgbaston.

In the first two Tests he averaged nine, in the next three 69. In the first two Tests he took two catches and six wickets, in the last three six catches and 18 wickets.

Nobody is ever going to believe that it was not the direct result of his being relieved of the captaincy, so one might as well accept it.

Brearley's most important contribution, apart from leaving Botham free for other things, was probably in restoring confidence and handling affairs so shrewdly in the two tight finishes at Headingley and Edgbaston. If margins of 18 runs and 29 runs had been the other way, Australia would have led 3-0.

NOT ALWAYS FIT

Another influential factor was that the equable pitches of other years, which might have favoured the young fit Australian fast bowlers, did not materialise – and in any case the younger Australian bowlers were not always all that fit.

The unlucky loss of Lawson and Hogg through injury put too much of a burden on Lillee and Alderman. Willis, by contrast, surpassed all hopes.

Who would have thought when he returned broken down again from Trinidad in February that he would have taken 25 wickets in the first five Tests here, bowling at times as fast as ever!

In one other department first appearances deceived. It had looked as if Australia's batting might have greater depth. Yet some decisive contributions came from England's later batsmen, Dilley and Old at Headingley, Emburey at Edgbaston, Knott, Allott and Emburey here.

Anyhow it has been a memorable series which has captured the public imagination as few others have in modern times. The honours may mostly have gone England's way, to selectors as well as players, but it takes two well matched sides to make a series like this and this one was close enough to be decided by one man, Ian Botham.

FIFTH TEST   FIFTH DAY

The Scoreboard

England: First innings
231
Second innings:
404
Australia: First innings
130
Second innings:

G. M. Wood, c Knott, b Allott	6
J. Dyson, run out	5
K. J. Hughes, lbw, b Botham	43
G. N. Yallop, b Emburey	14
A. R. Border, not out	23
M. F. Kent, c Brearley, b Emburey	2
R. W. Marsh, c Knott, b Willis	47
R. J. Bright, c Knott, b Willis	5
D. K. Lillee, c Botham, b Allott	28
T. M. Alderman, lbw, b Botham	0
M. R. Whitney, c Gatting, b Willis	0
Extras (lb 9, w 2, nb 18)	29

Total 402

Fall of wickets: 1-7, 2-24, 3-119, 4-198,
5-206, 6-296, 7-322, 8-373, 9-378.

Bowling	O	M	R	W
Willis	30.5	2	96	3
Allott	17	3	71	2
Botham	36	16	86	2
Emburey	49	9	107	2
Gatting	3	1	13	0

Man of the Match: I. T. Botham.
Umpires: D. J. Constant & K. G. Palmer.

England won by 103 runs

Sixth Test
THE OVAL
27 AUGUST – 1 SEPTEMBER 1981

Gooch a Doubt, but Big Changes May Be Delayed

Although England are 3-1 up in the Test series and the Ashes have been retained, the home selectors have only slightly more freedom this weekend when they choose the team for the final match against Australia at the Oval.

A Test match is still a Test match, and it would devalue the occasion and belittle the opposition to pick other than what is hoped will prove the strongest side.

Graham Gooch, surely certain to be needed in India, may be rested, for though staunch and successful against the fastest of bowling in other series, he has made only 139 runs in 10 innings.

He is one of the younger generation of batsmen who have high ability, but need technical adjustment after facing a surfeit of fast bowling on often uncertain pitches. In between times, the feverish unorthodoxy of much limited-over cricket has given them indifferent practice.

Gower, loosely, and Gatting, with a sudden excess after playing well, have been getting out after having done the hard work of playing themselves in. But at 24, their best years lie ahead.

The time may have come to review Geoffrey Boycott's position and his value as an anchor with the arrival of a younger one in Tavare.

Boycott averages only 25 in this series, but if spin is as dominant in India, as it was until a few years ago, he would make hundreds of runs there.

CASE FOR BARCLAY

The younger batsmen most likely to be fitted in at the Oval are Paul Parker and Wayne Larkins, although there is a case for trying John Barclay, who would be a fifth bowler and a second spinner.

So in the long term, the real problem is going to be finding bowlers. In the short term, there are enough batsmen in waiting to blood one or two at the Oval.

I doubt if the bowling will be changed here, though there may be several new bowlers in India. Paul Allott not only bowled respectably on what, in the second innings, became the most lifeless pitch of the series, but strengthened the later

102

batting with his straight method and placid temperament.

As for Bob Willis, if the series would not have have been won without Ian Botham, it would not have been won so quickly without Willis. At 32 he is still so much faster and more effective than others that it would be hard to have a genuine Test side at the moment without him.

It is a great joy that Alec Bedser's last season as chairman of selectors, but not I trust his last as a selector, should have been blessed by success.

No-one could have served with more devotion and, if the committees under his chairmanship made mistakes, as all committees do, how many more might they have made but for his commonsense and high standards?

He has won a series in a season of acutely difficult decisions, with the help of some unpredictable pitches on which the England batsmen made just enough runs and the expected limitations of the bowling were covered up. It will not always be so.

24 AUGUST 1981

Gooch & Gower Replaced by Larkins & Parker

England have made two changes in their batting for the final Cornhill Test at the Oval on Thursday, bringing in Paul Parker for his first match and Wayne Larkins, instead of David Gower and Graham Gooch.

In a way, the changes are made out of strength rather than weakness, for there are plenty of young batsmen worth a chance and not many bowlers, though the future in that department has become brighter this summer.

Chris Old, who had to withdraw from the 12 at Old Trafford through injury, is included again instead of Derek Underwood, no doubt after the selectors had taken a close look at a pitch unlikely to offer much to the spinner.

It is hard to believe that Gooch and Gower will not be needed in India, though the competition for batting places there will be tough, especially if, as seems likely, Keith Fletcher goes as captain and occupies one of them.

Gooch and Gower have probably suffered from a surfeit of fast bowling in the last two years, though they have played it well.

Fast-medium bowling on not always reliable English pitches has presented different problems. Gooch has not played straight enough against the moving ball; Gower has not used his feet enough.

In this series Gooch has made only 139 runs in 10 innings, including 44 on the best pitch at Lord's.

TIME FOR REST

Gower made 89 at Lord's, but in six of his 10 Test innings he has been out in the 20s and this points, I suppose, to a lack of concentration or too much recent Test cricket, which are added reasons for resting him.

Parker has been close to selection for several seasons, kept out partly, perhaps, because of a reluctance by the selectors to throw in new young batsmen against almost unrelieved fast bowling. It is a help that he is in the same brilliant class as Gower in the covers and further afield.

He will be the 27th Cambridge Blue to play Test cricket since the war, which testifies, among other things, to the value of good true pitches such as those produced by Cyril Coote at Fenner's.

It was on one of these that Parker announced himself in only his third first-class match by making 215 against Essex early in 1976.

The choice between Larkins, who has played in five Tests with a highest score of 33, and his Northamptonshire captain and opening partner, Geoff Cook, must have been a delicate one.

When the chairman of selectors saw them bat last Wednesday, Cook looked more what was wanted at the moment. He plays very straight.

The attraction of Larkins is doubtless that if he does become established he will have the strokes to offset the more dogged qualities of Boycott and Tavare. He is also an athletic fielder.

DETERMINED BOYCOTT

Boycott, very properly, I think, stays on until it has been confirmed that some younger opening batsman has the same sober determination not to give his wicket away easily.

104

To some extent he has been complementary to the younger more dashing school of batsmen who, except for Tavare, have tended to play some fine strokes followed all too soon by one not so fine.

Allott is retained after bowling respectably at Old Trafford, on what became latterly the most unhelpful pitch of the series, and after making an invaluable 52 not out in the first innings.

ACCURATE OLD

Whether he will play this time is doubtful for Old's experience and accuracy may be important if the pitch is as true as expected.

If Allott did not play, the side would again have only four bowlers. The selectors have been unlucky that the all-rounders of three years ago, such as Miller and Edmonds, have not trained on and that none of the batsmen bowls as effectively as, say, d'Oliveira used to.

On the other hand, if they can call on Botham, they are not all that unlucky.

---

27 AUGUST 1981

Prolific Wellham Set for Australia Debut: Hogg Pulls Out

There was no scent of anti-climax in the air at the Oval yesterday, as crowds queued for tickets for today's final Cornhill Test. Surrey announced that £182,000 had already been taken.

The two sides made various adjustments, partly through injury. Rodney Hogg dropped out through a cartilage injury in the morning, and Chris Old, who suffered a muscular spasm on Tuesday, pulled up sore after bowling at the nets in the afternoon. Mike Hendrick is standing by.

Australia, like England, will have a batsman new to Test cricket. While Paul Parker, brought in with Wayne Larkins, makes a long foreseen first appearance for England, Dirk Wellham, 22, replaces John Dyson, Australia's opening batsman.

Wellham, who will bat in the middle of the order, from where Kent will move up to open with Wood, first came on the scene when making 95 for the Combined Universities against England in Adelaide in November 1979.

It looked this summer as if he would be the unlucky batsman to be found on most tours, but he has worked his way into the Test side by making a lot of runs against the counties.

CHARITY CENTURY

This seems to have given much pleasure in Cranleigh, Surrey. During the Lord's Test the Australians were asked if they would like to send any spare players needing practice to perform in a charity match at Cranleigh on the Sunday.

Wellham turned up and made 100 and a lot of friends. He followed it with 100 against Northamptonshire next weekend, since when he has not looked back.

Some mild concern was caused yesterday, when Ian Botham arrived with a suspicion of water on the knee, but it will not stop his playing in a Test match in which he could leave a few more statistical landmarks behind.

NEAR LANDMARK

He needs 42 runs and eight wickets to become, at the age of 25, only the third player, after Benaud and Sobers, to score 2,000 runs and take 200 wickets in Test matches.

I am afraid that after his recent exploits too much may be expected of his batting. He has made a sensible reconnaissance at the start of most innings this summer, but anyone who plays as he does, even though he hits very straight, needs plenty of luck, especially early on.

28 AUGUST 1981

After euphoria comes toil for subdued England

Australia put in by Brearley, started the final Cornhill Test at the Oval yesterday by making 251 for four in a day's play which was more like what one would have expected before the singular events and euphoria of the last three Tests!

On a cloudless day and good pitch they batted without many worries. England bowled and fielded well, but made limited impact.

Every so often Australia had some accident, all of them involving the inevitable Botham, who took three wickets and held one of his most spectacular catches.

The day ended with Allan Border, 51 not out, batting ominously soundly and the England bowlers toiling for the last 85 minutes without looking much like breaking his stand with the youthful Wellham.

Yet England did concede only 52 runs in that period, helped by fielding in which Parker was outstanding, and they will have a ball only four overs old with which to start refreshed this morning.

UNUSUAL CHOICE

I doubt if it would have occurred to many past England captains to choose to field in these conditions, and in the short term it was not a success.

Wood and Kent made 120 for the first wicket before Botham removed them in successive overs, and this is Australia's highest opening stand for 55 Tests.

However judgment on these matters is usually best reserved until both sides have batted – and even later.

England's decision to put Australia in was probably prompted by the expectation that a hard, bouncy pitch might be at its liveliest on the first day and that the ball might swing on a lovely, hazy, late summer's morning.

I thought that with the new ball they bowled better than at any corresponding time in the series – and at lunch Australia were 85 for no wicket. Virtue is not always rewarded.

Australia did have two bits of luck in Willis's second and third overs. Kent, before scoring, was surprised by a ball which lifted and lobbed up off the bat into an empty space in the gully. Wood, when one, mis-hooked and skied the ball to a great height off the top edge.

Knott, followed by Brearley, set off in pursuit but failed to reach it and it looked as if Larkins at long-leg might have been nearer the eventual point of descent.

Thereafter, Wood and Kent played some fine strokes, Kent hitting hard off the back foot. Occasionally a ball kicked

107

unexpectedly, occasionally they played and missed and they were not at their best against Emburey, who came on after an hour.

But by the early afternoon this had developed into the most realistic Test match of the summer, and all went well for Australia until 50 minutes after lunch, when Botham bowled the left-handed Wood a short ball which he shaped to hook.

GENTLE CATCH

The ball was slanting away from Wood and, as it left him off the pitch, he realised that the projected hook was not a great idea. Too late he stopped his stroke. The ball flew gently off the face of the bat to Brearley, running back from first-slip.

In Botham's next over Kent played forward firmly without moving quite to the pitch of the ball. The stroke was uppish and well enough timed to carry to mid-off, where Gatting took a low catch.

Hughes and Yallop were soon playing with the same confidence as the first pair and added 44 in an hour. Though Brearley must by now have been pondering how his four bowlers were to be nursed through the rest of a hot day, he gave the gallant Willis another spell for the benefit of Yallop.

The fifth ball of Willis's last over before tea seemingly had Yallop undecided as to whether to go forward or back and he edged it fast and high above Botham at third-slip.

With the advent of Tavare, Botham had moved there from second-slip, where he has taken most of his catches, and leaping high he held a magnificent catch at the full extent of his right arm.

Willis had the athletic Parker stationed at backward square-leg for the uppish hook, but Border, like Yallop earlier, played the stroke just wide of him. Border was soon driving Emburey twice in an over for four, and Hendrick came on, passing Hughes's bat more than once.

Thirty runs had been added in half an hour when Hughes was out in a weird way. He had pulled a shortish ball from Botham towards the midwicket boundary when, in completing the stroke, his left foot touched the leg-stump, dislodging a bail.

Hughes had run two when the bad news was broken to him by umpire Bird at square-leg. It was as if the bail, noting that half an hour had passed since Botham was last involved in anything remarkable, had fallen off as a matter of form.

Border, when 23, played a ball on the walk to Gatting, a very close square short-leg, and only just thrust his bat back in time as Gatting threw down the wicket. Otherwise, he played thoroughly well, emphasising how lucky England had been to have disposed of him cheaply earlier in the series.

Wellham came through a cautious start against Emburey and it was beginning to look as if weary bowlers might be in for a bad last hour when Emburey and Hendrick recovered the initiative.

For the last 12 minutes Botham, taking the new ball in his 25th over, and Willis replaced them, and the day ended with honours still fairly even.

The Scoreboard

Australia: First innings

G. M. Wood, c Brearley, b Botham	66
M. F. Kent, c Gatting, b Botham	54
K. J. Hughes, hit wkt, b Botham	31
G. N. Yallop, c Botham, b Willis	26
A. R. Border, not out	51
D. M. Wellham, not out	19
Extras (b 1, lb 2, nb 1)	4

Total (4 wkts) 251

Fall of wickets: 1-120, 2-125, 3-169, 4-199.

Bowling	O	M	R	W
Willis	20	3	66	1
Hendrick	24	6	51	0
Botham	26	6	77	3
Emburey	21	2	53	0

Umpires: H. D. Bird & B. J. Meyer.

Teams – Sixth Test

England: Boycott, Larkins, Tavare, Gatting, Brearley, Parker, Botham, Knott, Emburey, Willis, Hendrick
Australia: Wood, Kent, Hughes, Yallop, Border, Wellham, Marsh, Bright, Lillee, Alderman, Whitney

Tourists Checked then Boycott Leads Response

England took Australia's last six wickets for 101 yesterday and, having bowled them out for 352 on an immaculate pitch, made their way prudently to 100 for one under the guidance of Boycott.

The difference between the first and second days of this last Cornhill Test of the series was that yesterday the ball swung. With Botham bowling well again, this is a great help to England and he wheeled away unchanged from the pavilion end.

When the innings ended he had taken six for 125. It is the 17th time in only 41 Tests that he has taken five wickets or more in an innings.

Willis's wonderfully sustained effort on this pitch, four for 91 in 31 overs, was equally worthy and Hendrick and Emburey, though they took no wickets, helped to keep order when the other two needed a rest. Willis duly reached a record of 110 wickets against Australia to better Wilfred Rhodes' tally.

Allan Border was undefeated at the end of the innings as he was at Old Trafford. Sound in defence, judicious in attack, he played just as well as he did there. He is a very formidable player now.

He is the first Australian to have made two hundreds in successive innings against England since Bill Lawry in 1965-66. Before that, a third left hander Arthur Morris made three in a row in 1946-47.

FIERY SPELL

England lost Larkins in the evening but not before he had batted very well in an opening stand which produced 61 at three runs an over and was the highest by England in the series. Thereafter, Boycott and Tavare, if not very strong on the entertainment side, did the job of consolidation staunchly.

England had a profitable morning helped by the fact that the late summer haze did not lift as it had on Thursday. Botham swung the ball from the start and reducing his pace and maintaining a full length he bowled admirably for two hours 50 minutes to the end of the innings, 21 overs for 48 runs and three wickets.

At the other end Willis bowled as fiery an opening spell as the pitch allowed him and in his third over Wellham, having started by playing back, went forward too late and was bowled by a ball which came back to him. Border, then 53 and otherwise in no trouble, was not far off being caught by wide mid-on off Botham at the same score, 260.

England's fielding was as good as at anytime in the series with Parker's running and throwing a joy to watch. Marsh was soon hooking Willis hard but, playing him rather firm footed, gave a catch to Tavare at second slip.

Whether or not disconcerted by a glimpse of Botham beginning to move across in front of him from third slip Tavare knocked the ball forward. Luckily by then Botham had arrived to catch the rebound.

Bright spent nearly 45 minutes over three runs before Botham in a splendid piece of bowling, produced a slower ball which swung more than most away from the bat and had him caught low down at first slip by Brearley.

There followed a mysterious piece of cricket in which at various times Border and Lillee seemed to be sheltering each other from the bowling. Nothing much happened until the first over after lunch when Willis brought his sixth ball back through a considerable gap between Lillee's bat and pad.

Botham was allowed two balls at the end of an over at Alderman and for the second produced an inswinger which hit the stumps off the pad. Border, 80 when Whitney arrived, went on refusing singles until the fifth or sixth balls of each over and eventually reached, in four hours 35 minutes, the 100 which had always seemed probable.

The last wicket stand added 32 and was not ended until Emburey pinned Border down and ensured that Whitney started an over facing Botham.

BRISKER PACE

Whitney scored his first runs in Test cricket after a total of 80 minutes in discreet support of Border here and at Old Trafford and was then bowled by Botham.

As long as Lillee and Alderman did not swing the ball as much as Botham had, England at this point had done pretty well. One's sympathies hereabout lay with Gooch and Gower who had batted on some awkward pitches in the previous Tests and were now going to miss a really true one.

Australia, too, were unlucky to be without Lawson who might have had the pace and strength to have had the same sort of effect on this pitch which Willis had had.

111

Boycott and Larkins had an hour's batting before tea which they negotiated safely. Lillee, Alderman and Whitney were brisker in pace than Botham and thus more straightforward. Perhaps the new ball swung less than its predecessor anyhow.

After tea Larkins, with most of the strike, played some fine strokes through the covers off the back foot against both Lillee and Alderman and was going well when Lillee thumped in a shorter faster ball which he edged to second slip.

After another over Lillee gave way to Whitney, who along with Bright, was soon being shown the full face of Tavare's bat. Whitney did have one moment of hope when Boycott, then 29, edged him low to second slip where Alderman, diving forward and to his left, just failed to pick up a half chance.

Otherwise Boycott played very safely, while Tavare dug in amid comment from a crowd which at that time in the evening scarcely appreciated the fact that he was doing exactly the job for which he was picked – providing an orthodox method and stability at No. 3.

In any case, England made 71 after tea compared with the 52 which Australia scored in two more overs on Thursday evening amid relatively little criticism.

The Scoreboard

Australia: First innings

G. M. Wood, c Brearley, b Botham	66
M. F. Kent, c Gatting, b Botham	54
K. J. Hughes, hit wkt, b Botham	31
G. N. Yallop, c Botham, b Willis	26
A. R. Border, not out	106
D. M. Wellham, b Willis	24
R. W. Marsh, c Botham, b Willis	12
R. J. Bright, c Brearley, b Botham	3
D. K. Lillee, b Willis	11
T. M. Alderman, b Botham	0
M. J. Whitney, b Botham	4
Extras (b 4, lb 6, w 1, nb 4)	15

Total 352

Fall of wickets: 1-120, 2-125, 3-169, 4-199, 5-260, 6-280, 7-303, 8-319, 9-320.

Bowling	O	M	R	W
Willis	31	6	91	4
Hendrick	31	·8	63	0
Botham	47	13	125	6
Emburey	23	2	58	0

England: First innings

F. Boycott, not out	47
W. Larkins, c Alderman, b Lillee	34
C. J. Tavare, not out	8
Extras (lb 2, nb 9)	11
Total (1 wkt)	100

Fall of wicket: 61

Bowling

	O	M	R	W
Lillee	11	1	33	1
Alderman	13	1	30	0
Whitney	8	2	15	0
Bright	11	5	11	0

Umpires: H. D. Bird & B. J. Meyer

31 AUGUST 1981

Fletcher Choice Puts Pressure on Batting Places

As the final Cornhill Test paused yesterday – before resuming its splendidly unpredictable course at the Oval with Australia leading by 74 runs with eight second innings wickets standing – the England selectors, less unpredictably, announced Keith Fletcher as captain for the winter tour of India and Sri Lanka.

No other good player with comparable experience of captaincy has emerged this season. As a successful captain of Essex since 1974, Fletcher, at 37, is the senior county captain after Mike Brearley – who is not available – and has been on two previous tours of India.

His second, in 1976-77, was not as successful as the first four years earlier, but there were reasons for that – a mid-tour injury, the hammering which he and others had received from Lillee and Thomson in Australia two years earlier, and the changed type of pitch encountered.

As a highly proficient player of spin, he was relatively less effective on pitches with more life and pace, but with six Tests due this time, it is hard to believe that some pitches will not be of the old slow type requiring Fletcher's skill against the turning ball.

HARMONIOUS PARTNERSHIP

At the end of that tour Fletcher played the last of his 56 Tests in the Centenary Match in Melbourne. His cricket thinking is highly regarded by his contemporaries and I have no doubt that

113

his partnership with Raman Subba Row, the manager, will be a harmonious one.

The snag, of course, as has been long foreseen, is that Fletcher takes up a batting place at a time when there are several young batsmen of promise and ability competing for the six places usually available for specialist batsmen on an Indian tour.

Now there are seven candidates for only five places – Boycott, Gooch, Tavare, Gower, Gatting, Larkins and Parker. Two are going to be unlucky, probably the last two unless they do something remarkable in the second innings of the present Test.

If anyone had suggested at three o'clock on Saturday after-noon – when England were 246 for two – that 10 wickets would fall for 104 runs in the remaining 2½ hours play, he would not have been taken seriously.

Yet this proved to be not quite the supremely easy batting pitch which it had seemed it might become. More satisfactorily it rewarded good bowling as well as good batting and the result depends on how much of each lies ahead.

Boycott played an invaluable innings lasting seven hours 20 minutes for his 21st Test hundred and Tavare – briefly and fluently – and Gatting in a third-wicket stand of 115 helped him to steer England to a position of enviable strength.

By delaying taking the new ball for five overs so that Lillee and Alderman could have the tea interval to refresh themselves after 40 minutes, Hughes, like everyone else on the packed ground, seemed to be looking ahead to an innings lasting for a long time.

Yet from Gatting's misjudgment in playing no stroke to Lillee's first ball, everything changed. Lillee and Alderman moved the new ball enough and made it bounce enough to upset the middle batting and they took four wickets in 4.2 overs which also included a missed catch at first slip offered by Boycott when 121.

Boycott's fine innings ended with one of the catches of the year by Yallop leaping high to his right in the gully.

SEVEN FOR LILLEE

After Knott had kept Australia's lead down to 38 with strokes of his own and Lillee had taken his seventh wicket – surprising-ly for the first time in a Test innings – England had 55 minutes' bowling.

Botham was running up warily as he does when bothered by

his back, but he took his 199th Test wicket with a good ball which had Kent well caught by Brearley at first slip.

Hendrick was assigned the last over of the day and when his fourth ball had Hughes lbw, the scene was set very promisingly for another absorbing and fluctuating day today.

The Scoreboard

Australia: First innings

352

Second innings:

G. M. Wood, not out			20
M. F. Kent, c Brearley, b Botham			7
K. J. Hughes, lbw, b Hendrick			6
Extras (lb 1, nb 2)			3

Total (2 wkts) 36

Fall of wickets: 1-26, 2-36.

Bowling	O	M	R	W
Willis	3	0	12	0
Botham	5	1	18	1
Hendrick	4.4	2	2	1
Emburey	1	0	1	0

England: First innings:

G. Boycott, c Yallop, b Lillee	137
W. Larkins, c Alderman, b Lillee	34
C. J. Tavare, c Marsh, b Lillee	24
M. W. Gatting, b Lillee	53
J. M. Brearley, c Bright, Alderman	0
P. W. G. Parker, c Kent, b Alderman	0
I. T. Botham, c Yallop, b Lillee	3
A. P. E. Knott, b Lillee	36
J. E. Emburey, lbw, b Lillee	0
R. G. D. Willis, b Alderman	3
M. Hendrick, not out	0
Extras (nb 12, lb 9, w 3)	24

Total 314

Fall of wickets: 1-61, 2-131, 3-246, 4-248, 5-248, 6-256, 7-293, 8-293, 9-302.

Bowling	O	M	R	W
Lillee	31.4	4	89	7
Alderman	35	4	84	3
Whitney	23	3	76	0
Bright	21	6	41	0

Umpires: H. D. Bird & B. J. Meyer.

1 SEPTEMBER 1981

Wellham Century Puts Injury-hit England on Rack

Australia's recovery from a start of 41 for three may prove today to have been rather too much of a good thing, for it leaves them 382 runs ahead of

England with only six hours of the final Cornhill Test remaining.

For England to win, they would have to set up a record to eclipse all the others in this series, for the highest they have ever made to win a series in this country is the 263 for nine against Australia here at the Oval in 1902.

Australia may still win today, but if they had declared with an hour to go, leaving England to make about 330 in nearly seven hours, the English batsmen might have felt more committed to round off the series today by taking chances which would have eased Australia's task.

It is not certain that the light would have been fit for the start of an innings and in that last hour Australia did have the satisfaction of seeing Dirk Wellham, their newest batsman, reach a fine hundred in his first Test.

A 22 year old schoolmaster who was playing only his 21st first-class innings, Wellham, admirably straight and orthodox, did nothing to let down Sir Donald Bradman's view expressed last year that he was the best of his generation in Australia.

He batted for 4½ hours and was dropped at 18 and 99 but he played with a composure and forthrightness unusual in one of his slim experience.

In many ways the biggest surprise about yesterday's events was that they had not occurred earlier this summer.

The fear that one day England's venerable bowlers and an overworked Botham would find themselves struggling in various stages of unfitness on a good batting pitch must have often nagged at the selectors, especially when they picked only four bowlers.

Yesterday the bad dreams came true. Only Emburey was fully fit and although Botham's particular injury merely reduced him to plugging away valiantly and indefinitely at medium pace, Willis retired for good in mid-afternoon, having aggravated a rib injury suffered while batting at Old Trafford.

It would not have been so bad if the catches had stuck, but apart from Wellham's escapes, Marsh was let off twice by Knott in a rugged innings of 52.

HENDRICK GETS WOOD

England made a deceptively promising start to the day. Hendrick finished the over in which he had had Hughes lbw on Saturday and, with the first ball of his next, produced one which lifted and left Wood to have him caught at the wicket.

116

Yallop and Border then played so discouragingly well that they made 60 in the next hour, but, at 104 Yallop dragged a ball from Hendrick onto his stumps.

Neither Willis nor Botham looked in the most robust health, although Botham kept going at medium pace and swung the ball enough in one over to make Border edge him short of first slip and to come close to bowling him between bat and pad.

The only other moment England looked like taking another wicket in the morning was in the last over, when Wellham – having played a superb straight drive off the back foot – mis-hit Botham off his toes to Willis at mid-on, who dropped the catch. If held, it would have removed Wellham for 18 and made the score 131 for five.

Wellham, in his first Test, had already looked a batsman of high promise, playing firmly forward or back, timing his strokes cleanly, including a spanking hook off Botham.

If he had a little trouble against Willis and the ball lifting chest high, he survived it and Willis left the field for the second time, leaving England's bowling looking fragile again.

Nothing seemed more certain than that Border was going to make his third successive Test hundred. By three o'clock England had bowled at him unavailingly for nearly 15 hours since Gower held a brilliant catch off Botham in the first innings at Old Trafford.

At that point, however, he went forward to Emburey, without quite reaching the pitch of the ball and gave a sharp catch, which Tavare, at slip, took well – almost behind the wicketkeeper.

ASTONISHING ESCAPE

After tea, Marsh had an astonishing escape. Called by Wellham for a sharp run on the off side he would have been out by five yards if Knott had gathered the throw from the bowler, Emburey, at the base of the stumps.

Marsh was then 15. When he was 40, Knott obliged again. In Botham's first over with the new ball. Marsh hooked and gave a straightforward catch which reached Knott chest high and was dropped.

This delayed yet again Botham's 200th Test wicket, but eventually Marsh pulled him over mid-wicket and Gatting, running back, judged the catch well. Only Grimmett and Lillee have reached 200 Test wickets in fewer than Botham's 41 Tests.

Wellham bore down fast on his hundred with some splendid

hooking and cutting off the tired bowlers, but when 99 drove Hendrick to Boycott at mid-off. Boycott dropped the catch.

UNNERVING EXPERIENCE

After this unnerving experience Wellham struggled for 25 minutes before he made the last run, which suited England, although by now the chances of a declaration had receded with the fading light.

Bright was bowled swinging across Botham, whom Wellham eventually hit for four off the back foot to become the 12th Australian batsman to make a hundred in his first Test, but the first to do so in England since Harry Graham in 1893.

Two balls later Botham, in his 37th over of the day, had him lbw and walked wearily away to third slip. Even there he was not finished, for in the remaining over he caught Whitney.

The Scoreboard

Australia: First innings
352

Second innings:

G. M. Wood, c Knott, b Hendrick	21
M. F. Kent, c Brearley, b Botham	7
K. J. Hughes, lbw, b Hendrick	6
G. N. Yallop, b Hendrick	35
A. R. Border, c Tavare, b Emburey	84
D. M. Wellham, lbw, b Botham	103
R. W. Marsh, c Gatting, b Botham	52
R. J. Bright, b Botham	11
D. K. Lillee, not out	8
M. J. Whitney, c Botham, b Hendrick	0
Extras (b 1, lb 8, w 1, nb 7)	17

Total (9 wkts) 344

Fall of wickets: 1-26, 2-36, 3-41, 4-104,
  5-205, 6-291, 7-332, 8-343, 9-344.

Bowling	O	M	R	W
Willis	10	0	41	0
Botham	42	9	128	4
Hendrick	29.2	6	82	4
Emburey	23	3	76	1

England: First innings
314

Umpires: H. D. Bird & B. J. Meyer.

Brearley & Knott Hold on to Deny Australia

An historic series ended with another stirring finish yesterday evening as England hung on at the Oval to draw the final Cornhill Test which they had looked like losing earlier in the day.

Alan Knott was still there at the end, having batted for the final 2¾ hours, for much of it with Mike Brearley. If this is the last of Brearley's Test innings, it was also one of his best.

When they began their partnership, England were 144 for six with two hours 40 minutes left or, as it proved, 48 overs.

The stand lasted for nearly two hours and survived seven of the final 20 overs against Bright, Yallop and Whitney. Lillee and Alderman were kept in reserve partly because the light was not always good enough, partly because they had the new ball due for the final 10 overs.

The light improved and Lillee, brought back for the eighth over, had Brearley caught at the wicket for once playing unnecessarily outside the off stump.

EMBUREY DROPPED

Thereafter Emburey did everything required of him – with just one bad moment in the 18th over when he was dropped at fifth slip off Lillee. With only Willis and Hendrick to come, the catch, if taken, could still have decided the match.

Lillee bowled yesterday faster than for much of the summer and at his very best. He was named as Man of the Match, in which he had taken 11 wickets. The Man of the Series, of course, was Botham.

It may not have been one of Brearley's most brilliant ideas to put Australia in on the best batting pitch of the series which occasionally showed justified signs of wear yesterday. But it is fair to say that Australia bowled better on it, which was what one always expected, and with more pitches like this they would doubtless not be going home as 3-1 losers.

At 10.30 yesterday morning it looked as if a well-organised defence would be needed and that was most likely to come from Boycott and Tavare. But after 50 minutes both were out, Boycott lbw when Lillee brought the fourth ball of the day back to him. Tavare was caught at first slip off one which Whitney slanted across him.

BREEZY GATTING

At 18 for two Gatting breezed in and addressed himself to the situation entirely differently. Within a few minutes the fast bowlers were being driven off front foot and back with rare zest and though there was a 10-minute stoppage for bad light, he went in for lunch having made 46 out of 65 in an hour.

In the half-hour after lunch the picture changed. In the fourth over Larkins, who had batted soundly for two hours 10 minutes, met a ball from Lillee which lifted sharply to have him caught at second slip.

Any difficulties which Gatting had had were against Bright bowling in the rough outside his leg stump, but four overs later Lillee produced almost the same ball as to Larkins and Kent took the catch at first slip.

Parker stayed for nearly an hour and seemed to be settling down when Alderman bowled him a good ball which left him. Instinctively he followed it and Kent took another catch.

BOTHAM BRIEF

Botham would not be everybody's choice as a batsman to play out the last 3¼ hours for a draw. He was soon banging the ball about and skying it just over deep mid-off with a stroke aimed at mid-wicket.

His end after making 16 in 10 minutes was that of a somewhat weary hero, lbw to Alderman inswinging towards midwicket and missing a ball which kept rather low. It was Alderman's 42nd wicket of the series, beating Rodney Hogg's 41 of 1978-79 as the best for an Australian bowler against England.

It proved to be his last, for Brearley and Knott took over in their widely contrasting ways.

Brearley played very straight with the occasional well timed off-drive. Knott ranged from painstaking defence to cutting, carving and sweeping. The policy had clearly been for every one to play his natural game – and it worked.

The Scoreboard

Australia: First innings:
352
Second innings:
344-9 dec.
England: First innings:
314
Second innings:

G. Boycott, lbw Lillee	0
W. Larkins, c Alderman, b Lillee	24
C. J. Tavare, c Kent, b Whitney	8
M. W. Gatting, c Kent, b Lillee	56
P. W. G. Parker, c Kent b Alderman	13
J. M. Brearley, lbw, b Lillee	51
I. T. Botham, lbw, b Alderman	16
A. P. E. Knott, not out	70
J. E. Emburey, not out	5
Extras (b 2, w 5, nb 2)	18

Total (7 wkts) 261

Fall of wickets: 1-0, 2-18, 3-88, 4-101,
    5-127, 6-144, 7-237.

Bowling	O	M	R	W
Lillee	30	10	70	4
Alderman	19	6	60	2
Whitney	11	4	46	1
Bright	27	12	50	0
Yallop	8	2	17	0

Umpires: H. D. Bird & B. J. Meyer.

Match Drawn

EDITORIAL

Summer Wine

One would have almost preferred to lose the Sixth Test. The great Dennis Lillee may not succeed in getting a fleur de lys stitched beside the Southern Cross on the Australian flag. But such talent and long-hauling resolution deserved consummation. One is glad that the series has ended with Australia taking a decent share of the glory, for it has been a glorious series, indeed a wonderful year for cricket. We antique souls with 'V' necked pullovers and briar pipes who for some years have seemed to be participating in an arcane ritual abstracted from the Golden Bough – a sort of midsummer druidry – find ourselves joined at sold-out grounds by the broad masses. Who would have thought a little time ago, when Mr Kerry Packer had put cricket into tights (well at any rate pink pads), that the new boredom of the empty grounds under floodlights might be replaced by a normal cricket which managed to be so exciting that great numbers were turned away?

We have had a splendid synthesis of the cavalier cricket of Botham and the Roundhead cricket of Boycott. We have seen a spin bowler, Ray Bright, getting batsmen out round their legs in a way which was supposed to have gone out with civilisation. There has been the very best kind of old fashioned captaincy from Brearley – humane, persuasive and well-mannered. We have seen a major new batsman in Allan Border who is turning into the key Australian player. The wicket-keeping has been excellent. One could go on. Alas one *is* going on – becoming quite bufferish. Well God stand up for buffers! The shades of football are falling fast. We have been put upon and much mocked for as long as we can remember as celebrants of a dying delight, butterflies of a summer parenthesis but latterly such dull, boring butterflies. Somehow we are in the fashion again. And in all candour the greatest share of credit must go to Botham. Most recent batting has been like Dr Johnson's remark about the Giant's Causeway – worth seeing, but not worth going to see. Those fiery centuries have created, for the first time in ages, an England star whom people will travel great distances to watch.

The bad times for Ian Botham. A costly mishap in the First Test. Allan Border, the only Australian to exceed 20 in the first innings, survives a fast but catchable chance when 17. He went on to make 63.

Two old protagonists on the lively pitch at Headingley. Geoffrey Boycott has to take a ball from Dennis Lillee on the back.

Right: The turning-point. With England apparently within minutes of an innings defeat in the Third Test, Graham Dilley, destined to make 56, launches a counter-attack soon to be turned into cricket history by Ian Botham.

Left: Botham, dominant again, driving Alderman high and straight during his 149 not out at Headingley.

Right: Bob Willis in his match-winning spell of eight for 43 in the last innings at Headingley.

Willis yorks Bright, Australia are out for 111 and England have won the Third Test which 24 hours earlier they had apparently been losing by an innings.

A vital wicket. Chris Old brings a ball back to bowl Allan Border off the inside edge and Australia are 65 for five in their last innings at Headingley.

Ian Botham listens to his captain but seems doubtful. Mike Brearley said later that Botham was diffident about coming on for the spell which brought him five wickets for one run and gave England the Fourth Test by 29 runs.

Left: Edgbaston on the first afternoon of the Fourth Test. Willis batting against Alderman during a last wicket stand with Old which added 24 precious runs. He was out in Alderman's next over.

Old Trafford, first day. Border at second slip catches Emburey to make England 137 for eight. The joy of Hughes and Kent was to some extent premature, for Border broke a finger in taking the catch. He still made 123 not out in the second innings.

Left: The end of the Fourth Test. Alderman is yorked by Botham.

Chris Tavare and his individual grip on the bat at Old Trafford where he
ended the run of failures by England's number three batsmen.

Left: Terry Alderman at Old Trafford during one of the marathon spells
which ultimately brought him an Australian record of 42 wickets in a series
against England.

Ian Botham sweeps Bright for four to reach his historic 100 at Old Trafford.

Right: Allan Border during the innings of 123 not out which held up England for 6¾ hours in the second innings of the Fifth Test despite a broken finger in his left hand.

The captains reflect what they feel about it all as they go into lunch at the Oval on the last day of the series. Brearley is adding a match-saving 51 to his previous triumphs.

The Series in Figures

BY BILL FRINDALL

123

FIRST TEST   ENGLAND FIRST INNINGS

ENGLAND 1st INNINGS v AUSTRALIA 1st TEST at TRENT BRIDGE, NOTTINGHAM on 18,19,20,21 JUNE, 1981.   TOSS: AUSTRALIA

IN	OUT	MINS	No.	BATSMAN	HOW OUT	BOWLER	RUNS	WKT	TOTAL	6s	4s	BALLS	NOTES ON DISMISSAL
11·00	11·18	18	1	GOOCH	c WOOD	LILLEE	10	1	13	·	2	18	Edged outswinger to 1st slip.
11·00	12·22	82	2	BOYCOTT	c BORDER	ALDERMAN	27	3	57	·	1	53	Edged outswinger to 2nd slip.
11·20	11·29	9	3	WOOLMER	c WOOD	LILLEE	0	2	13	·	·	9	Lifting ball - gloved high to 1st slip (2-handed catch).
11·31	12·36	65	4	GOWER	c YALLOP	LILLEE	26	4	67	·	4	39	Cut short malish ball to 4th slip/gully.
12·24	3·35	154	5	GATTING	LBW	HOGG	52	8	159	·	6	117	Missed hook - ball kept low.
12·38	1·50	35	6	WILLEY	c BORDER	ALDERMAN	10	5	92	·	1	22	Edged away-seamer to 2nd slip.
1·52	2·07	15	7	BOTHAM *	BOWLED	ALDERMAN	1	6	96	·	·	8	Aimed on-drive at outswinger started on leg stump - middle stump hit.
2·09	2·44	35	8	DOWNTON †	c YALLOP	ALDERMAN	8	7	116	·	·	23	Edged low to 4th slip.
2·46	3·57	71	9	DILLEY	BOWLED	HOGG	34	10	185	·	6	49	Missed hit to leg across ball that hit his off-stump.
3·36	3·37	1	10	WILLIS	c MARSH	HOGG	0	9	159	·	·	8	First-ball - edged leg-glance.
3·38	(3·57)	19	11	HENDRICK	NOT OUT		6			·	1	8	

EXTRAS   b - lb 6 w 1 nb 4   = 11   0⁶ 21⁴   347 balls (inc. 7 no balls)

TOTAL   185 all out at 3.57 pm   (off 56.4 overs in 260 MIN.)

* CAPTAIN   † WICKET-KEEPER

BOWLER	O	M	R	W
LILLEE	13	3	34	3
ALDERMAN	24	7	68	4
HOGG	11·4	1	47	3
LAWSON	8	3	25	0
			11	
	56·4	14	185	10

Alderman's first spell in Test cricket (figures 3-51) - 24-7-68-4.

HRS	OVERS	RUNS	RUNS	MINS	OVERS	LAST 50 (in mins)
1	13	33	50	77	16·5	77
2	13	50	100	156	34·2	79
3	14	30	150	227	50·1	71
4	13	47				

13 OVERS 0 BALLS / HOUR
3·26 RUNS/OVER
53 RUNS/100 BALLS

WKT	PARTNERSHIP		RUNS	MINS
1st	Gooch	Boycott	13	18
2nd	Boycott	Woolmer	0	9
3rd	Boycott	Gower	44	51
4th	Gower	Gatting	10	12
5th	Gatting	Willey	25	35
6th	Gatting	Botham	4	15
7th	Gatting	Downton	20	35
8th	Gatting	Dilley	43	49
9th	Dilley	Willis	0	1
10th	Dilley	Hendrick	26	19
			185.	

LUNCH: 87-4 (GATTING 10*, WILLEY 10*) OFF 27 OVERS IN 123 MINUTES

TEA INTERVAL TAKEN AT END OF INNINGS

AUSTRALIA 1ˢᵀ INNINGS

IN REPLY TO ENGLAND'S 185 ALL OUT

IN	OUT	MINS	No.	BATSMAN	HOW OUT	BOWLER	RUNS	WKT	TOTAL	6s	4s	BALLS	NOTES ON DISMISSAL
4.17	4.18	1	1	WOOD	LBW	DILLEY	0	1	0	·	·	2	Played back to breakback.
4.17	5.18	61	2	DYSON	Cᵗ WOOLMER	WILLIS	5	2	21	·	·	45	Fended short ball to short leg.
4.20	5.24	64	3	YALLOP	BOWLED	HENDRICK	13	3	21	·	·	47	Beaten by faster inswinger.
5.20	6.02	42	4	HUGHES *	LBW	WILLIS	7	4	33	·	1	34	WILLIS'S 200ᵀᴴ TEST WICKET Beaten by breakback.
5.26	4.29	122	5	CHAPPELL	BOWLED	HENDRICK	17	5	64	·	1	80	Off stump - drove across leg-cutter.
11.00	11.30	266	6	BORDER	Cᵗ AND BOWLED	BOTHAM	63	10	179	·	7	204	Fast return catch from straight drive.
4.31	4.52	21	7	MARSH †	Cᵗ BOYCOTT	WILLIS	19	6	89	·	3	13	Skier - long leg - well-judged catch. Top-edged hook.
4.54	5.24	30	8	LAWSON	Cᵗ GOWER	BOTHAM	14	7	110	·	1	18	Drove outswinger to cover.
5.26	6.23	57	9	LILLEE	Cᵗ DOWNTON	DILLEY	12	8	147	·	1	48	Edged away - seamer.
6.25	6.35	10	10	HOGG	Cᵗ BOYCOTT	DILLEY	0	9	153	·	·	7	Chopped simple catch to wide mid-on.
6.37	(11.30)	51	11	ALDERMAN	NOT OUT		12	·	·		·	31	-
				EXTRAS	b 4 lb 8	w 1 nb 4	17						

0ᵇ 15⁴   529 balls (inc 8 no balls)

TOTAL (OFF 86.5 OVERS IN 371 MIN) 179

* CAPTAIN   † WICKET-KEEPER

14 OVERS 0 BALLS/HOUR
2.06 RUNS/OVER
34 RUNS/100 BALLS

BOWLER	O	M	R	W
DILLEY	20	7	38	3
WILLIS	30	14	47	3
HENDRICK	20	7	43	2
BOTHAM	16.5	6	34	2
			17	
	86.5	34	179	10

HRS	OVERS	RUNS
1	14	21
2	14	17
3	13	19
4	13	48
5	16	30
6	14	36

	RUNS	MINS	OVERS	LAST 50 (in mins)
	50	155	35.1	155
	100	236	53.3	81
	150	315	73.1	79

STUMPS: 33-4   CHAPPELL 5* (36 min)
(1ST DAY)   OFF 24.5 OVERS IN 105 MINUTES
2ND DAY: RSP at 11.32 am   41-4   73 min. LOST
LUNCH: 41-4   CHAPPELL 6*   BORDER 6*
TAKEN AT 12.45   OFF 31 OVERS IN 137 MINUTES
RESTARTED at 1.35 (10 MIN LOST - 8.5 TOTAL LOST)
RSP at 2.00 pm
TEA: 51-4   CHAPPELL 12*, BORDER 10*
TAKEN at 3.40 pm   OFF 36.3 OVERS IN 162 MIN (18.3 LOST)
STUMPS: 166-9   BORDER 51* (235 min.)   ALDERMAN 7* (21 min.)
2ND DAY · 125 MIN (NET) LOST   OFF 79 OVERS IN 340 MIN

WKT	PARTNERSHIP		RUNS	MINS
1ˢᵗ	Wood	Dyson	0	1
2ⁿᵈ	Dyson	Yallop	21	58
3ʳᵈ	Yallop	Hughes	0	4
4ᵗʰ	Hughes	Chappell	12	36
5ᵗʰ	Chappell	Border	31	86
6ᵗʰ	Border	Marsh	25	21
7ᵗʰ	Border	Lawson	21	30
8ᵗʰ	Border	Lillee	37	57
9ᵗʰ	Border	Hogg	6	10
10ᵗʰ	Border	Alderman	26	51
				179

ENGLAND 2ND INNINGS

FIRST TEST   ENGLAND SECOND INNINGS

6 RUNS AHEAD ON FIRST INNINGS

IN	OUT	MINS	No.	BATSMAN	HOW OUT	BOWLER	RUNS	WKT	TOTAL	6s	4s	BALLS	NOTES ON DISMISSAL
11.40	11.50	10	1	GOOCH	c YALLOP	LILLEE	6	1	12	.	1	9	Cut hard to gully's left - magnificent catch.
11.40	11.59	16	2	BOYCOTT	c MARSH	ALDERMAN	4	2	12	.	1	9	Edged away - seamer.
11.52	11.59	7	3	WOOLMER	c MARSH	ALDERMAN	0	3	13	.	.	4	Edged away-seamer.
11.58	2.34	117	4	GOWER	c Sub (M.F. KENT)	LILLEE	28	6	94	.	3	72	"PAIR." MARSH'S 100TH DISMISSAL v ENG. Edged low to gully.
12.02	12.44	42	5	GATTING	LBW	ALDERMAN	15	4	39	.	2	34	Played back to breakback that kept low.
12.46	1.55	30	6	WILLEY	LBW	LILLEE	13	5	61	.	2	27	Missed breakback - dropped previous ball.
1.57	12.25	65	7	BOTHAM *	c BORDER	LILLEE	33	8	113	.	4	38	Edged low to 2nd slip - ball moved away slightly.
2.36	12.18	19	8	DOWNTON †	LBW	ALDERMAN	3	7	109	.	.	12	Played back - beaten by break back.
12.20	12.40	20	9	DILLEY	c MARSH	ALDERMAN	13	9	125	.	2	18	Gloved attempted pull — gentle skier.
12.27	12.47	20	10	WILLIS	c CHAPPELL	LILLEE	1	10	125	.	.	10	Skier to deep backward-point.
12.42	(12.47)	5	11	HENDRICK	NOT OUT		0			.	.	2	-
				EXTRAS	b -	lb 8	9	w -	nb 1				0ᵇ 15⁴ 235 balls (inc 3 no balls)

TOTAL (off 38.4 overs in 185 MIN.)   125 all out at 12.47 pm on 4th day.

* CAPTAIN   † WICKET-KEEPER

12 OVERS 3 BALLS/HOUR
3-23 RUNS/OVER
53 RUNS/100 BALLS

WKT	PARTNERSHIP		RUNS	MINS
1ST	Gooch	Boycott	12	10
2ND	Boycott	Woolmer	0	4
3RD	Woolmer	Gower	1	1
4TH	Gower	Gatting	26	42
5TH	Gower	Willey	22	30
6TH	Gower	Botham	33	37
7TH	Botham	Downton	15	19
8TH	Botham	Dilley	4	5
9TH	Dilley	Willis	12	13
10TH	Willis	Hendrick	0	5
			125	

LUNCH: 44-4   GOWER 12* (62 min.) WILLEY 0* (14 min.)
OFF 17 OVERS IN 80 MINUTES

B.LSP at 2.37 - followed by heavy drizzle.

TEA: 94-6   BOTHAM 21*, DOWNTON 0*
OFF 29.1 OVERS IN 138 MINUTES

STUMPS (3RD DAY)   183 MIN LOST 3RD DAY.
PLAY ABANDONED at 5.50 pm.

4TH DAY: ENGLAND added 31 runs in 47 minutes for the loss of their last 4 wkts.

ALDERMAN 9 - 130 in his first Test

LILLEE took 5 wickets in an innings for the 18th time in 49 Tests.

BOWLER	O	M	R	W
LILLEE	16.4	2	46	5
ALDERMAN	19	3	62	5
HOGG	3	1	8	0
			9	
	38.4	6	125	10

HRS	OVERS	RUNS	RUNS	MINS	OVERS	LAST 50 (in mins)
1	12	35	50	93	19.5	93
2	13	47	100	143	30.2	50

AUSTRALIA 2ND INNINGS   REQUIRING 132 RUNS TO WIN IN A MINIMUM OF 663 MINUTES

IN	OUT	MINS	No.	BATSMAN	HOW OUT	BOWLER	RUNS	WKT	TOTAL	6s	4s	BALLS	NOTES ON DISMISSAL
12·57	4·01	145	1	DYSON	C' DOWNTON	DILLEY	38	4	80	.	1	89	Edged lifting away - seamer.
12·57	1·28	31	2	WOOD	C' WOOLMER	WILLIS	8	1	20	.	1	28	Bat/pad catch to short square leg.
1·30	2·52	42	3	YALLOP	C' GATTING	BOTHAM	6	2	40	.	.	34	Edged outswinger low to 3rd slip's left - great diving catch.
2·54	3·52	58	4	HUGHES *	LBW	DILLEY	22	3	77	.	3	53	Drove across the line.
3·54	(5·49)	94	5	CHAPPELL	NOT OUT		20			.	.	65	Made winning hit.
4·03	5·28	65	6	BORDER	BOWLED	DILLEY	20	5	122	.	2	49	Played outside breakback.
5·30	5·32	2	7	MARSH †	LBW	DILLEY	0	6	122	.	.	2	Played across line.
5·34	(5·49)	15	8	LAWSON	NOT OUT		5			.	1	11	-
			9	LILLEE	} Did not bat								
			10	HOGG									
			11	ALDERMAN									

EXTRAS   b 1 lb 6 6 w - nb 6   = 13   of 8s   331 balls (inc 6 no balls)

TOTAL   132 - 6   (OFF 54·1 OVERS IN 232 MIN.)

* CAPTAIN   † WICKET-KEEPER

BOWLER	O	M	R	W
DILLEY	11·1	4	24	4
WILLIS	13	2	28	1
HENDRICK	20	7	33	0
BOTHAM	10	1	34	1
		13		
	54·1	14	13 2	6

HRS	OVERS	RUNS
1	13	29
2	16	37
3	13	34

RUNS	MINS	OVERS	LAST 50 (in mins)
50	100	24	100
100	179	41·5	79

14 OVERS 0 BALLS/HOUR
2·44 RUNS/OVER
40 RUNS/100 BALLS

WKT	PARTNERSHIP		RUNS	MINS
1st	Dyson	Wood	20	31
2nd	Dyson	Yallop	20	42
3rd	Dyson	Hughes	37	58
4th	Dyson	Chappell	3	7
5th	Chappell	Border	42	65
6th	Chappell	Marsh	0	2
7th	Chappell	Lawson	10*	15
			132	

LUNCH : 32 - 1   DYSON 16* (63 min.)   YALLOP 3* (30 min.)
AUSTRALIA REQUIRE 100 TO WIN   off 14 overs in 63 min.

TEA : 106 - 4   CHAPPELL 10* (46 min.)   BORDER 12* (37 min.)
AUSTRALIA REQUIRE 26 TO WIN   off 43 overs in 183 min.

AUSTRALIA won by 4 WICKETS at 5.49 pm on the 4th day (Sunday).
AUSTRALIA'S FIRST VICTORY AT TRENT BRIDGE SINCE 1948.   TOTAL TIME LOST (NET) : 5 hr 8 min.

MAN OF THE MATCH : D.K. LILLEE
Adjudicator : T.W. GRAVENEY

SECOND TEST ENGLAND FIRST INNINGS

ENGLAND 1ST INNINGS v. AUSTRALIA (2ND TEST) at LORD'S, LONDON on JULY 2,3,4,6,7, 1981. TOSS: AUSTRALIA

IN	OUT	MINS	No.	BATSMAN	HOW OUT	BOWLER	RUNS	WKT	TOTAL	6s	4s	BALLS	NOTES ON DISMISSAL
11.30	12.44	74	1	GOOCH	c' YALLOP	LAWSON	44	1	60	.	6	53	Mistimed hook at attempted bouncer. Gentle mid-wkt catch
11.30	1.08	98	2	BOYCOTT	c' ALDERMAN	LAWSON	17	2	65	.	3	62	Edged to 3rd slip via 2nd slip (BORDER). Back-foot push.
12.46 / 5.36	2.23 / 5.24	116	3	WOOLMER	c' MARSH	LAWSON	21	(2)1 / 9	83 / 258	.	3	82	Retired hurt when 13' - arm bruised by ball from Lawson. Gloved attempt at hook.
1.10	4.48	124	4	GOWER	c' MARSH	LAWSON	27	3	134	.	4	86	Faint edge - followed lifting offside ball.
2.34	6.17	168	5	GATTING	LBW	BRIGHT	59	4	187	.	9	137	HS in TESTS. Pushed across 'arm' ball.
4.50	5.34	246	6	WILLEY	c' BORDER	ALDERMAN	82	5	284	.	12	181	Edged to 2nd slip - two-handed catch to his left.
6.19	5.48	171	7	EMBUREY	Run out [LILLEE? / MARSH]		31	6	293	.	.	124	Attempted second run to long-leg.
5.50	5.56	6	8	BOTHAM *	LBW	LAWSON	0	7	293	.	.	3	Hit across good-length straight ball.
5.58	6.01	3	9	TAYLOR †	c' HUGHES	LAWSON	0	8	293	.	.	4	Short ball hit glove - diving catch at short leg.
6.03	(6.35)	32	10	DILLEY	NOT OUT		7			.	1	21	-
6.26	6.35	9	11	WILLIS	c' WOOD	LAWSON	5	10	311	.	.	4	Edged on-drive to 1st slip.
				EXTRAS	b 2 lb 3		18						

TOTAL b 2 lb 3 w 3 nb 10 (OFF 124.1 OVERS IN 532 MIN.) = 311

0 6s 36 4s 757 balls (inc. 12 nb)
311 all out at 6.35pm 2ND DAY

14 OVERS 0 BALLS/HOUR
2.50 RUNS/OVER
41 RUNS/100 BALLS

WKT	PARTNERSHIP		RUNS	MINS
1st	Gooch	Boycott	60	74
2nd	Boycott	Woolmer	5	22
3rd	Woolmer	Gower	18*	68
	Gatting		51	79
4th	Gatting	Willey	53	87
5th	Willey	Emburey	97	157
6th	Emburey	Woolmer	9	12
7th	Woolmer	Botham	0	6
8th	Woolmer	Taylor	0	3
9th	Woolmer	Dilley	5	21
10th	Dilley	Willis	13	9
			311	

LUNCH: 78-2 WOOLMER 9* (45 min), GOWER 6* (21 min) OFF 26 OVERS IN 121 MINUTES

BLSP 2.55 to 3.26. 88-2 (37 overs) 31 MIN. LOST

TEA: 119-2 47 OVERS 203 MIN. GOWER 14* (109 min), GATTING 24* (64 min)

STUMPS (1ST DAY): 191-4 OFF 77 OVERS IN 327 MINUTES WILLEY 25* (101 min), EMBUREY 0* (12 min)

RSP 11.45 to 2.42pm. LUNCH (at 1pm): 195-4. 157 MINUTES LOST. WILLEY 25*, EMBUREY 2* OFF 81 OVERS IN 342 MINUTES

RSP 4.15 TEA: 260-4 (102.4 OVERS IN 435') WILLEY 44* EMB. 22

ENGLAND lost last 6 wickets for 27 runs in 59 minutes off 76 balls.

BOWLER	O	M	R	W
LILLEE	35.4	7	102	0
ALDERMAN	30.2	7	79	1
LAWSON	43.1	14	81	7
BRIGHT	15	7	31	1
			18	1
	124.1	35	311	10

2ND NEW BALL taken at 2.59 pm 2nd day - ENGLAND 200-4 after 85 overs.

HRS	OVERS	RUNS	RUNS	MINS	OVERS	LAST 50 (in mins)
1	14	54	50	58	13.2	58
2	12	24	100	177	40	119
3	15	23	150	253	57.4	76
4	13	39	200	357	84.5	104
5	16	43	250	416	98.2	59
6	15	17	300	524	122.3	108
7	14	50				
8	15	40				

* CAPTAIN † WICKET-KEEPER

AUSTRALIA 1ˢᵗ INNINGS   IN REPLY TO ENGLAND'S 311 ALL OUT

SECOND TEST   AUSTRALIA FIRST INNINGS

IN	OUT	MINS	No.	BATSMAN	HOW OUT	BOWLER	RUNS	WKT	TOTAL	6s	4s	BALLS	NOTES ON DISMISSAL
6.47	12.54	61	1	WOOD	c⁺ TAYLOR	WILLIS	44	1	62	.	5	59	Breakback took inside edge - superb right-handed catch.
6.47	12.57	64	2	DYSON	c⁺ GOWER	BOTHAM	7	2	62	.	.	30	Edged outswinger to 2nd slip
12.56	1.11	15	3	YALLOP	BOWLED	DILLEY	1	3	69	.	.	7	Played on - beaten by pace and breakback.
12.59	4.00	141	4	HUGHES *	c⁺ WILLIS	EMBUREY	42	5	167	.	5	118	Skied straight-drive to deep mid-off. Falling catch.
1.13	1.30	17	5	CHAPPELL	c⁺ TAYLOR	DILLEY	2	4	81	.	.	13	Failed to avoid lifting ball (flicked gloves).
2.10	5.58	208	6	BORDER	c⁺ GATTING	BOTHAM	64	6	244	1	8	164	Edged square cut to 2nd slip.
4.02	11.44	143	7	MARSH †	LBW	DILLEY	47	7	257	.	9	116	Padded up to breakback - 3rd ball with new ball.
6.00	1.05	126	8	BRIGHT	LBW	EMBUREY	33	9	314	.	4	97	Hts in Tests Missed sweep.
11.46	12.15	29	9	LAWSON	LBW	WILLIS	5	8	268	.	1	22	Beaten by breakback.
12.17	(2.44)	107	10	LILLEE	NOT OUT		40			.	5	86	-
1.07	2.44	57	11	ALDERMAN	c⁺ TAYLOR	WILLIS	5	10	345	.	.	42	Gloved fast lifting ball.
				EXTRAS	b 6 lb 11	w 6 nb 32	55				1⁶ 37.	754 balls (inc. 42 no balls)	

TOTAL   345 all out at 2.44 pm 4th DAY.
(off 118.4 OVERS in 492 min.)

LEAD: 34

* CAPTAIN   † WICKET-KEEPER

14 OVERS 3 BALLS/HOUR
2.91 RUNS/OVER
46 RUNS/100 BALLS

WKT	PARTNERSHIP		RUNS	MINS
1st	Wood	Dyson	62	61
2nd	Dyson	Yallop	0	1
3rd	Yallop	Hughes	7	12
4th	Hughes	Chappell	12	17
5th	Hughes	Border	86	110
6th	Border	Marsh	77	96
7th	Marsh	Bright	13	45
8th	Bright	Lawson	11	29
9th	Bright	Lillee	46	48
10th	Lillee	Alderman	31	57
			345	

B.I.S.P at 6.59pm 151 MINUTES (NET) LOST 2ND DAY
WOOD 6⁴, DYSON 3⁴ OFF 2.3 OVERS IN 12 MIN

STUMPS (2ND DAY): 10-0

RESTART DELAYED 35 MIN.
LUNCH: 81-4   OFF 26 OVERS IN 97 MIN.   HUGHES 14⁴ (31 MIN)

TEA: 172-5   BORDER 37⁴ (120 MINUTES), MARSH 5⁴ (8 MINUTES) OFF 49 OVERS IN 217 MIN.
139 BEHIND

STUMPS: 253-6   MARSH 42⁴ (129 MINUTE), BRIGHT 3⁴ (31 MINUTES) OFF 81 OVERS IN 338 MIN.
3RD DAY

LUNCH: 328-9   LILLEE 28⁴ (75min.), ALDERMAN 4⁴ (23 min.) OFF 110 OVERS IN 458 MIN.

BOWLER	O	M	R	W
WILLIS	27.4	9	50	3
DILLEY	30	8	106	3
BOTHAM	26	8	71	2
GOOCH	10	4	28	0
EMBUREY	25	12	35	2
			55	
	118.4	41	345	10

2ND NEW BALL taken at 11.42am, 4TH DAY
- AUSTRALIA 257-6 after 85 overs

RUNS	MINS	OVERS	LAST (in mins)
50	43	8.4	43
100	113	24.4	70
150	180	40.1	67
200	246	58.2	66
250	328	78.2	82
300	415	100	87

HRS	OVERS	RUNS
1	12	61
2	14	45
3	14	43
4	17	49
5	14	41
6	16	18
7	14	50
8	14	31

ENGLAND 2ND INNINGS

34 RUNS BEHIND ON FIRST INNINGS

IN	OUT	MINS	No.	BATSMAN	HOW OUT	BOWLER	RUNS	WKT	TOTAL	6s	4s	BALLS	NOTES ON DISMISSAL
2:55	3:35	40	1	GOOCH	LBW	LAWSON	20	1	31	·	2	32	Played back - beaten by breakback.
2:55	12:20	279	2	BOYCOTT	c MARSH	LILLEE	60	3	178	·	5	211	His 60th TEST FIFTY (= RECORD) Steered wide ball to keeper's right
3:37	4:39	43	3	WOOLMER	LBW	ALDERMAN	9	2	55	·	2	38	Late on yorker.
4:41	1:52	245	4	GOWER	c ALDERMAN	LILLEE	89	5	217	1	11	207	Lifting ball 'stopped' - gully catch via bat shoulder.
12:22	1:50	48	5	GATTING	c WOOD	BRIGHT	16	4	217	1	·	44	Edged to slip via pad.
1:51	1:57	6	6	BOTHAM *	BOWLED	BRIGHT	0	6	217	·	·	1	First ball - "PAIR" Missed sweep - bowled behind legs.
1:53	2:22	29	7	WILLEY	c CHAPPELL	BRIGHT	12	7	242	·	1	20	Skied back foot drive to cover.
1:59	(2:40)	41	8	DILLEY	NOT OUT		27			·	3	38	-
2:23	2:40	17	9	TAYLOR †	BOWLED	LILLEE	9	8	265	·	1	16	Drove across a yorker.
			10	EMBUREY	did not bat								
			11	WILLIS									
				EXTRAS	b 2 lb 8	w - nb 13	23						
				TOTAL			23				4s 24	607 balls (inc 15 no balls)	

265-8 DECLARED at 2:40pm 5th DAY
(off 98.4 overs in 380 min)

* CAPTAIN † WICKET-KEEPER

BOWLER	O	M	R	W
LILLEE	26.4	8	82	3
ALDERMAN	17	2	42	1
LAWSON	19	6	51	1
BRIGHT	36	18	67	3
			23	
	98.4	34	265	8

2ND NEW BALL NOT TAKEN

HRS	OVERS	RUNS
1	13	40
2	15	51
3	16	31
4	17	28
5	15	38
6	17	49

RUNS	MINS	OVERS	LAST 50 (in mins)
50	78	17.3	78
100	149	35.4	71
150	240	61	91
200	323	84	83
250	372	96.4	49

15 OVERS 3 BALLS/HOUR
2.69 RUNS/OVER
44 RUNS/100 BALLS

WKT	PARTNERSHIP		RUNS	MINS
1st	Gooch	Boycott	31	40
2nd	Boycott	Woolmer	24	43
3rd	Boycott	Gower	123	193
4th	Gower	Gatting	39	48
5th	Gower	Botham	0	1
6th	Botham	Willey	0	4
7th	Willey	Dilley	25	23
8th	Dilley	Taylor	23	17
			265	

TEA: 48-1

STUMPS: 129-2   BOYCOTT 13s (76 minutes) / WOOLMER 5s (34 min)
OFF 17 OVERS IN 76 MIN.

4TH DAY   BOYCOTT 47s (200 min) / GOWER 38s (113 min)
OFF 50 OVERS IN 200 MIN

LUNCH: 197-3   GOWER 77s (233 min) / GATTING 9s (38 min)
LEAD: 163   OFF 83 OVERS IN 320 MIN.

BEFORE LUNCH: 68 RUNS in 120 MIN. OFF 33 OVERS
AFTER LUNCH: 68 RUNS in 60 MIN OFF 15.4 OVERS

AUSTRALIA 2ND INNINGS

SET TO SCORE 232 RUNS IN A MINIMUM OF 170 MINUTES

IN	OUT	MINS	No.	BATSMAN	HOW OUT	BOWLER	RUNS	WKT	TOTAL	6s	4s	BALLS	NOTES ON DISMISSAL
2.50	2.56	6	1	DYSON	LBW	DILLEY	1	1	2	.	.	6	Played across yorker - hit on foot.
2.50	(5.58)	168	2	WOOD	NOT OUT		62			.	6	131	-
2.58	3.25	27	3	YALLOP	C BOTHAM	WILLIS	3	2	11	.	.	32	Edged low to 2nd slip.
3.28	4.05	17	4	HUGHES *	LBW	DILLEY	4	3	17	.	.	13	Played half-forward - misjudged line.
4.07	5.13	66	5	CHAPPELL	C TAYLOR	BOTHAM	5	4	62	.	.	69	Edged forward push.
5.16	(5.58)	42	6	BORDER	NOT OUT		12			.	1	46	-
			7	MARSH †									
			8	BRIGHT									
			9	LAWSON	Did not bat								
			10	LILLEE									
			11	ALDERMAN									
				EXTRAS	b - lb - w 1 nb 2		3						
				TOTAL	(off 48.5 overs in 168 minutes)		**90-4**			0^6	7^4	297 balls (including 4 no balls)	

* CAPTAIN   † WICKET-KEEPER

BOWLER	O	M	R	W
WILLIS	12	3	35	1
DILLEY	7.5	1	18	2
EMBUREY	21	10	24	0
BOTHAM	8	3	10	1
			3	
	48.5	17	90	4

HRS	OVERS	RUNS	RUNS	MINS	OVERS	LAST 50 (in mins)
1	16	17	50	97	26.3	97
2	18	43				

TEA: 15-2

WKT	PARTNERSHIP		RUNS	MINS
1st	Dyson	Wood	2	6
2nd	Wood	Yallop	9	27
3rd	Wood	Hughes	6	17
4th	Wood	Chappell	45	66
5th	Wood	Border	28*	42
			90	

17 OVERS 2 BALLS/HOUR
1.84 RUNS/OVER
30 RUNS/100 BALLS

WOOD 8*, HUGHES 2* OFF 13 OVERS IN 50 MIN.

MATCH DRAWN

ENGLAND'S 12th MATCH WITHOUT VICTORY (equalling their longest run of non-success)

MAN OF THE MATCH: G.F. LAWSON (Adjudicator: A.R. LEWIS)

TOTAL TIME LOST (NET): 3 HRS 17 MIN.

THIRD TEST — AUSTRALIA FIRST INNINGS

AUSTRALIA 1st INNINGS v. ENGLAND (3RD TEST) at HEADINGLEY, LEEDS on JULY 16,17,18,20,21, 1981. TOSS: AUSTRALIA

IN	OUT	MINS	No.	BATSMAN	HOW OUT	BOWLER	RUNS	WKT	TOTAL	6s	4s	BALLS	NOTES ON DISMISSAL
11.00	6.42	294	1	DYSON	BOWLED	DILLEY	102	3	196	·	14	234	Hit across yorker – leg stump. HS in TESTS
11.00	12.19	71	2	WOOD	LBW	BOTHAM	34	1	55	·	4	55	Beaten by inswing – played back. Botham's 3rd ball
12.21	5.43	161	3	CHAPPELL	C' TAYLOR	WILLEY	27	2	149	·	2	135	Top-edged cut at long-hop. HS in TESTS
5.44	4.57	270	4	HUGHES	C' AND BOWLED	BOTHAM	89	5	332	·	8	208	Edged gentle return catch.
6.44	12.03	48	5	BRIGHT	BOWLED	DILLEY	7	4	220	·	1	36	Middle and off stumps hit by outswinger.
12.04	5.44	208	6	YALLOP	C' TAYLOR	BOTHAM	58	7	357	·	5	167	Edged cut.
4.59	5.34	35	7	BORDER	LBW	BOTHAM	8	6	354	·	1	20	Beaten by late inswing.
5.36	6.41	65	8	MARSH	BOWLED	BOTHAM	28	9	401	·	5	50	Beaten by inswinging yorker.
5.46	6.31	45	9	LAWSON	C' TAYLOR	BOTHAM	13	8	396	·	2	35	Funked short ball – gentle leg-side catch.
6.33	(6.41)	8	10	LILLEE	NOT OUT		3			·	·	6	* umpires subsequently ruled that he was "not out D."
6.41	(6.41)	-	11	ALDERMAN	NOT OUT		0			·	·	-	Stopped on to field of play fractionally before declaration.
					EXTRAS	b 4 lb 13 w 3 nb 12	32			0	42		946 balls (including 14 no balls)

TOTAL 401-9 DECLARED at 6.41 pm 2nd day. (OFF 155.2 OVERS IN 609 MINUTES)

* CAPTAIN † WICKET-KEEPER

15 OVERS 2 BALLS/HOUR
2·58 RUNS/OVER
42 RUNS/100 BALLS

WKT	PARTNERSHIP		RUNS	MINS
1st	Dyson	Wood	55	71
2nd	Dyson	Chappell	94	161
3rd	Dyson	Hughes	47	58
4th	Hughes	Bright	24	48
5th	Hughes	Yallop	112	161
6th	Yallop	Border	22	35
7th	Yallop	Marsh	3	8
8th	Marsh	Lawson	39	45
9th	Marsh	Lillee	5	8
10th	Lillee	Alderman	0*	-
			401	

LUNCH: 60-1
8.50 at 12.26 pm
DYSON 20* (78 min) / CHAPPELL 0* (5 min)
OFF 18.5 OVERS IN 78 MINUTES
42 MINUTES LOST IN SESSION

TEA: 97-1
DYSON 43* (161 min) / CHAPPELL 11* (88 min)
110 MIN LOST (TOTAL) OFF 42 OVERS IN 161 MINUTES

STUMPS: 203-3
(1st DAY) (50' lost all day)
HUGHES 24* (79 min) / BRIGHT 1* (19 min)
OFF 82 OVERS IN 314 MINUTES

LUNCH: 250-4
HUGHES 46*, YALLOP 11*
OFF 102 OVERS IN 400 MIN

TEA: 309-4
HUGHES 81* YALLOP 34*
OFF 123 OVERS IN 478 MINUTES
2ND DAY: 46' lost (NLP)

BOWLER	O	M	R	W
WILLIS	30	8	72	0
OLD	43	14	91	0
DILLEY	27	4	78	2
BOTHAM	39.2	11	95	6
WILLEY	13	2	31	1
BOYCOTT	3	2	2	0
			32	
	155.2	41	401	9

2ND NEW BALL TAKEN at 11.10 am. 2nd day
– AUSTRALIA 214-3 after 85 overs.

HRS	OVERS	RUNS
1	15	50
2	15	26
3	17	31
4	17	47
5	14	42
6	15	33
7	14	34
8	16	46
9	16	45
10	14	42

RUNS	MINS	OVERS	LAST 50 (in mins)
50	61	15	61
100	164	42.4	103
150	238	62.4	74
200	302	79	64
250	396	101.5	94
300	461	118.1	65
350	530	136.2	69
400	605	154.4	75

ENGLAND 1st INNINGS   IN REPLY TO AUSTRALIA'S 401-9 DECLARED

THIRD TEST   ENGLAND FIRST INNINGS

IN	OUT	MINS	No.	BATSMAN	HOW OUT	BOWLER	RUNS	WKT	TOTAL	6s	4s	BALLS	NOTES ON DISMISSAL
6.52	11.06	17	1	GOOCH	LBW	ALDERMAN	2	1	12	·	·	7	Played across line to his first ball of third day.
6.52	12.19	89	2	BOYCOTT	BOWLED	LAWSON	12	3	42	·	·	58	Leg-stump via outside of left pad - played inside innings.
11.08	12.12	64	3	BREARLEY *	C MARSH	ALDERMAN	10	2	40	·	·	53	Edged defensive stroke to offside ball that lifted.
12.14	1.50	58	4	GOWER	C MARSH	LAWSON	24	4	84	·	3	50	Edged ball that lifted and moved away.
12.21	1.57	58	5	GATTING	LBW	LILLEE	15	5	87	·	2	29	Played forward - ball hit pad before bat.
1.52	2.21	29	6	WILLEY	BOWLED	LAWSON	8	6	112	·	·	22	Yorked via foot.
1.59	3.19	80	7	BOTHAM	C MARSH	LILLEE	50	8	166	·	8	54	Edged lifting away seamer. Marsh's 264th dismissal - Test Record
2.23	2.59	36	8	TAYLOR †	C MARSH	LILLEE	5	7	148	·	1	23	Followed short wide offside ball.
3.02	3.32	30	9	DILLEY	C and BOWLED	LILLEE	13	10	174	·	2	17	Simple return catch - checked drive.
3.21	3.25	4	10	OLD	C BORDER	ALDERMAN	0	9	167	·	·	4	Edged lifting ball to 2nd slip.
3.27	(3.32)	5	11	WILLIS	NOT OUT		1			·	·	4	-
				EXTRAS	b 6 lb 11 w 6 nb 11		34			0⁶	16⁴	321 balls (inc. 16 no balls)	

0⁶ 16⁴ → 0^6 16^4

TOTAL (OFF 50.5 OVERS IN 245 MIN) 174 all out at 3.32pm 3rd day (227 behind)

* CAPTAIN   † WICKET-KEEPER

BOWLER	O	M	R	W
LILLEE	18.5	7	49	4
ALDERMAN	19	4	59	3
LAWSON	13	3	32	3
	50.5	14	174	10

HRS	OVERS	RUNS
1	13	30
2	12	41
3	13	53
4	12	44

	RUNS	MINS	OVERS	LAST 50 (in mins)
	50	107	22.1	107
	100	166	35.2	61
	150	217	45	51

WKT	PARTNERSHIP		RUNS	MINS
1st	Gooch	Boycott	12	17
2nd	Boycott	Brearley	28	64
3rd	Boycott	Gower	2	5
4th	Gower	Gatting	42	50
5th	Gatting	Willey	3	5
6th	Willey	Botham	25	22
7th	Botham	Taylor	36	36
8th	Botham	Dilley	18	17
9th	Dilley	Old	1	4
10th	Dilley	Willis	7	5
			174	

12 OVERS 2 BALLS/HOUR
3.42 RUNS/OVER
54 RUNS/100 BALLS

STUMPS: 7-0   Gooch 2* Boycott 0* off 2 overs in 10 minutes

LUNCH: 78-3   Gower 24*; Gatting 9* off 28 overs in 132 min

TEA taken between innings

AUSTRALIA ENFORCED FOLLOW-ON

THIRD TEST   ENGLAND SECOND INNINGS

ENGLAND 2ND INNINGS   FOLLOWING ON 227 RUNS BEHIND ON FIRST INNINGS

IN	OUT	MINS	No.	BATSMAN	HOW OUT	BOWLER	RUNS	WKT	TOTAL	6s	4s	BALLS	NOTES ON DISMISSAL
3·53	3·55	2	1	GOOCH	c ALDERMAN	LILLEE	0	1	0	·	·	3	Edged low to 3rd slip who dived in front of 2nd slip.
3·53	2·52	215	2	BOYCOTT	LBW	ALDERMAN	46	6	133	·	1	141	Front foot - beaten by breakback.
5·00	11·16	33	3	BREARLEY *	c ALDERMAN	LILLEE	14	2	18	·	3	29	Edged low to 3rd slip - pushed forward to outswinger.
11·18	11·54	36	4	GOWER	c BORDER	ALDERMAN	9	3	37	·	1	22	Edged square-push to 2nd slip - didn't move his feet.
11·56	12·06	10	5	GATTING	LBW	ALDERMAN	1	4	41	·	·	10	Beaten by breakback that kept low - played back.
12·08	2·13	84	6	WILLEY	c DYSON	LILLEE	33	5	105	·	6	56	Cut short ball to short 3rd man. DILLEE'S 142nd WKT + ENG - beating TRUMBLE'S RECORD
2·13	(10·41)	219	7	BOTHAM	NOT OUT		149			·	27	148	7th off 87 balls. HS in Tests. 114 in boundaries
2·54	3·03	9	8	TAYLOR	† c BRIGHT	ALDERMAN	1	7	135	·	·	9	Fended short ball to forward short-leg.
3·04	4·44	80	9	DILLEY	BOWLED	ALDERMAN	56	8	252	·	9	75	Played on - edged vast drive. 1ST TEST FIFTY
4·46	5·40	54	10	OLD	BOWLED	LAWSON	29	9	319	·	6	31	Yorked leg stump by slower ball.
5·42	10·41	31	11	WILLIS	c BORDER	ALDERMAN	2	10	356	·	·	9	Edged to second slip.
				EXTRAS	b 5 lb 3 w 3 nb 5		16			1 6	53 4	533 balls (inc. 8 no balls)	
				TOTAL	(OFF 87·3 OVERS IN 396 MIN)		**356**		all out at 10·41 am 5th day				

13 OVERS 1 BALLS/HOUR
4·07 RUNS/OVER
67 RUNS/100 BALLS

WKT	PARTNERSHIP		RUNS	MINS
1st	Gooch	Boycott	0	2
2nd	Boycott	Brearley	18	33
3rd	Boycott	Gower	19	36
4th	Boycott	Gatting	4	10
5th	Boycott	Willey	64	84
6th	Boycott	Botham	28	38
7th	Botham	Taylor	2	9
8th	Botham	Dilley	117	80
9th	Botham	Old	67	54
10th	Botham	Willis	37	31
			356	

STUMPS (3RD DAY): 6-1	BOYCOTT 0* BREARLEY 4*		
ENGLAND 221 BEHIND	OFF 4·2 OVERS IN 21'		
LUNCH: 78-4	BOYCOTT 35* (143') WILLEY 12* (54')		
ENGLAND 149 BEHIND	OFF 32 OVERS IN 143'		
TEA: 176-7	BOTHAM 39* (96 min) DILLEY 25* (36 min)		
ENGLAND 51 BEHIND	OFF 58 OVERS IN 263 min		
STUMPS (4TH DAY)	BOTHAM 145* (208' 137') WILLIS 1* (20' 5b)		
351-9	OFF 85 OVERS IN 385 min LEAD·124		
345 RUNS SCORED ON FOURTH DAY			

BOWLER	O	M	R	W		HRS	OVERS	RUNS		RUNS	MINS	OVERS	LAST 50 (in mins)
LILLEE	25	6	94	3		1	14	23		50	96	22·3	96
ALDERMAN	35·3	6	135	6		2	12	32		100	170	38	74
LAWSON	23	4	96	1		3	14	53		150	242	53·1	72
BRIGHT	4	0	15	0		4	13	41		200	275	60·5	33
						5	13	90		250	305	67·2	30
			16			6	13	76		300	342	74·5	37
	87·3	16	356	10						350	385	84·5	43

2ND NEW BALL taken at 10·30am 5TH day
- ENGLAND 351-9 after 85 overs

* CAPTAIN † WICKET-KEEPER

AUSTRALIA 2ND INNINGS REQUIRING 130 RUNS IN A MINIMUM OF 339 MINUTES

IN	OUT	MINS	No.	BATSMAN	HOW OUT	BOWLER	RUNS	WKT TOTAL	6s	4s	BALLS	NOTES ON DISMISSAL
10.51	11.00	9	1	WOOD	C TAYLOR	BOTHAM	10	1 13	.	2	10	Edged drive at outswinger.
10.51	1.29	119	2	DYSON	C TAYLOR	WILLIS	34	6 68	.	3	83	Edged hook at bouncer.
11.02	12.10	68	3	CHAPPELL	C TAYLOR	WILLIS	8	2 56	.	.	56	Failed to avoid bouncer - gentle catch.
12.12	12.26	14	4	HUGHES *	C BOTHAM	WILLIS	0	3 58	.	.	9	Edged short ball low to 3rd slip.
12.28	12.30	2	5	YALLOP	C GATTING	WILLIS	0	4 58	.	.	3	Fended lifting ball to short square leg.
1.10	1.23	13	6	BORDER	BOWLED	OLD	0	5 65	.	.	8	Leg stump - vast break back.
1.24	1.42	18	7	MARSH †	C DILLEY	WILLIS	4	7 74	.	.	9	Hooked bouncer to long-leg - skier on boundary.
1.31	2.20	49	8	BRIGHT	BOWLED	WILLIS	19	10 111	.	2	32	Drove across middle stump yorker.
1.44	1.48	4	9	LAWSON	C TAYLOR	WILLIS	1	8 75	.	.	2	Followed lifting away seamer TAYLOR 1271 ct (WORLD RECORD)
1.50	2.12	22	10	LILLEE	C GATTING	WILLIS	17	9 110	.	3	15	Attempted to hook a bouncer - skier to mid-on.
2.14	(2.20)	6	11	ALDERMAN	NOT OUT		0		.	.	5	-
				EXTRAS	b - lb 3	w 1 nb 14	18		o^b 10^+		232 balls (inc. 15 no balls)	

TOTAL (OFF 36.1 OVERS IN 169 MINUTES) 111 all out at 2.20pm on 5th day.

* CAPTAIN † WICKET-KEEPER

12 OVERS 5 BALLS/HOUR
3.07 RUNS/OVER
48 RUNS/100 BALLS

WKT	PARTNERSHIP		RUNS	MINS
1st	Wood	Dyson	13	9
2nd	Dyson	Chappell	43	68
3rd	Dyson	Hughes	2	14
4th	Dyson	Yallop	0	2
5th	Dyson	Border	7	13
6th	Dyson	Marsh	3	5
7th	Marsh	Bright	6	11
8th	Bright	Lawson	1	4
9th	Bright	Lillee	35	22
10th	Bright	Alderman	1	6

LUNCH: 58-4 DYSON 29*
RUNS REQUIRED: 72 OFF 22.4 OVERS IN 99 MIN

ENGLAND won by 18 RUNS
- only the second time that a side has won after following on in Test cricket.

MAN OF THE MATCH: I.T. BOTHAM
ADJUDICATOR: F.S. TRUEMAN

TOTAL TIME LOST (NET): 3 HOURS 22 MIN.

HRS	OVERS	RUNS	RUNS	MINS	OVERS	LAST 50 (in mins)
1	14	39	50	73	17.1	73
2	13	32	100	156	33.5	83

BOWLER	O	M	R	W
BOTHAM	7	3	14	1
DILLEY	2	0	11	0
WILLIS	15.1	3	43	8
OLD	9	1	21	1
WILLEY	3	1	4	0
			18	
	36.1	8	111	10

135

FOURTH TEST   ENGLAND FIRST INNINGS

ENGLAND 1ST INNINGS v. AUSTRALIA 4TH TEST at EDGBASTON, BIRMINGHAM on JULY 30, 31, AUGUST 1, 2, 1981. TOSS: ENGLAND

IN	OUT	MINS	No.	BATSMAN	HOW OUT	BOWLER	RUNS	WKT	TOTAL	6s	4s	BALLS	NOTES ON DISMISSAL
11.30	12.14	44	1	BOYCOTT	c MARSH	ALDERMAN	13	1	29	.	1	42	Flicked at short away-seamer.
11.30	2.56	166	2	BREARLEY*	c BORDER	LILLEE	48	4	101	.	6	109	On 13 for 63 min. Edged drive at wide half-volley to 2nd slip.
12.16	12.26	10	3	GOWER	c HOGG	ALDERMAN	0	2	29	.	.	10	Mistimed hook at bouncer. 'dolly' to wide mid-on.
12.28	1.18	50	4	GOOCH	c MARSH	BRIGHT	21	3	60	.	3	43	Top-edged fierce square-cut. Bird deliberated.
1.20	3.29	89	5	GATTING	c ALDERMAN	LILLEE	21	5	126	.	2	46	Edged firm-footed off-drive to 3rd slip.
2.58	4.04	66	6	WILLEY	BOWLED	BRIGHT	16	6	145	.	2	59	Bowled behind legs sweeping at leg-break pitched in 'rough.'
3.31	4.49	58	7	BOTHAM	BOWLED	ALDERMAN	26	7	161	.	3	43	off-stump - Pushed outside break-back - through 'gate'.
4.06	5.05	39	8	EMBUREY	BOWLED	HOGG	3	9	165	.	.	33	Missed mid-wicket push - middle stump.
4.51	4.52	1	9	TAYLOR †	BOWLED	ALDERMAN	0	8	161	.	.	3	Played inside straight ball - off-stump.
4.54 (5.29)		35	10	OLD	NOT OUT		11	.	.	.	.	23	-
5.07	5.29	22	11	WILLIS	c MARSH	ALDERMAN	13	10	189	.	2	15	Chased short wide ball - caught in front of 1st slip.
				EXTRAS	b 1 lb 5 w 1 nb 10		17						

TOTAL (OFF 69.1 OVERS IN 300 MIN.) 189 all out at 5.29 pm.

0⁶ 19⁴ 426 balls (inc. 11 no balls)

13 OVERS 5 BALLS/HOUR
2.73 RUNS/OVER
44 RUNS/100 BALLS

* CAPTAIN   † WICKET-KEEPER

BOWLER	O	M	R	W
LILLEE	18	4	61	2
ALDERMAN	23.1	8	42	5
HOGG	16	3	49	1
BRIGHT	12	4	20	2
			17	
	69.1	19	189	10

	RUNS	MINS	OVERS	LAST 50 (in mins)
	50	97	21.1	97
	100	159	35.4	62
	150	245	57.2	86

HRS	OVERS	RUNS
1	14	30
2	13	38
3	14	45
4	15	33
5	13	43

LUNCH: 68-3

TEA: 146-6

BREARLEY 25* (120 min.) GATTING 0* (10 min.) OFF 27 OVERS IN 120 MIN.
BOTHAM 13* (40 min.) EMBUREY 0* (5 min.) OFF 56 OVERS IN 241 MIN.

WKT	PARTNERSHIP		RUNS	MINS
1st	Boycott	Brearley	29	44
2nd	Brearley	Gower	0	10
3rd	Brearley	Gooch	31	50
4th	Brearley	Gatting	41	36
5th	Gatting	Willey	25	31
6th	Willey	Botham	19	33
7th	Botham	Emburey	16	23
8th	Emburey	Taylor	0	1
9th	Emburey	Old	4	11
9th	Old	Willis	24	22

189

FOURTH TEST   AUSTRALIA FIRST INNINGS

AUSTRALIA 1ST INNINGS

IN REPLY TO ENGLAND'S 189 ALL OUT

IN	OUT	MINS	No.	BATSMAN	HOW OUT	BOWLER	RUNS	WKT	TOTAL	6s	4s	BALLS	NOTES ON DISMISSAL
5.41	2.15	174	1	WOOD	Run out (OLD)		38	4	115	.	2	139	Beaten by mid-off's direct hit on bowler's stumps.
5.41	5.55	14	2	DYSON	BOWLED	OLD	1	1	5	.	.	11	Beaten by late inswing - played back.
5.57	6.22	25	3	BORDER	C'TAYLOR	OLD	2	2	14	.	.	24	Faint defensive edge to last ball just outside off-stump.
6.24	12.27	63	4	BRIGHT	LBW	BOTHAM	27	3	62	.	.	51	Missed turn to leg - breakback.
12.29	3.01	112	5	HUGHES *	LBW	OLD	47	5	166	.	7	101	Misjudged line - played outside ball pitched on off stump.
2.16	3.54	98	6	YALLOP	BOWLED	EMBUREY	30	6	203	.	3	70	Beaten by flight - down wicket - driving.
3.03	5.12	109	7	KENT	C'WILLIS	EMBUREY	46	8	253	.	6	81	'Pick-up' shot hit hard to deep square-leg.
3.56	4.41	25	8	MARSH †	BOWLED	EMBUREY	2	7	220	.	.	24	Missed cut at 'arm' ball.
4.43	5.23	40	9	LILLEE	BOWLED	EMBUREY	18	10	258	.	3	43	Missed 'cow-shot'.
5.14	5.15	1	10	HOGG	Run out (BREARLEY)		0	9	253	.	.	0	Called for single to wide-mid-on by Lillee - direct throw.
5.17	(5.23)	6	11	ALDERMAN	NOT OUT		3			.	.	3	-
				EXTRAS	b 4 lb 19 w - nb 21		44			0⁶	25⁴		

TOTAL 258   all out at 5.23 pm 2nd day   547 balls (inc 26 no balls)

(OFF 86.5 OVERS IN 342 MIN.)

LEAD: 69

* CAPTAIN † WICKET-KEEPER

---

15 OVERS 1 BALLS/HOUR
2.97 RUNS/OVER
47 RUNS/100 BALLS

WKT	PARTNERSHIP		RUNS	MINS
1st	Wood	Dyson	5	14
2nd	Wood	Border	9	25
3rd	Wood	Bright	48	63
4th	Wood	Hughes	53	66
5th	Hughes	Yallop	51	45
6th	Yallop	Kent	37	51
7th	Kent	Marsh	17	25
8th	Kent	Lillee	33	29
9th	Lillee	Hogg	0	1
10th	Lillee	Alderman	5	6
				258

STUMPS: 19-2 (1st DAY)
WOOD 6" (45 min)
BRIGHT 0" (6 min)
OFF 11 OVERS IN 49 MINUTES

LUNCH: 111-3
WOOD 36* (169 min)
HUGHES 25* (61 min)
OFF 43 OVERS IN 169 MIN.

TEA: 217-6
KENT 30* (67 min)
MARSH 2* (14 min)
OFF 73 OVERS IN 289 MIN.

RUNS	MINS	OVERS	LAST 50 (in mins)
50	92	23.2	92
100	147	36	55
150	202	51.1	55
200	260	64.2	58
250	330	84	70

nb	HRS	OVERS	RUNS
28	1	14	24
-	2	15	53
1	3	16	42
4	4	14	58
5	5	17	42

BOWLER	O	M	R	W	nb
WILLIS	19	3	63	0	28
OLD	21	8	44	3	-
EMBUREY	26.5	12	43	4	1
BOTHAM	20	1	64	4	
			44	2	
	86.5	24	258	10	

2ND NEW BALL NOT TAKEN.

FOURTH TEST   ENGLAND SECOND INNINGS

69 RUNS BEHIND ON FIRST INNINGS

IN	OUT	MINS	No.	BATSMAN	HOW OUT	BOWLER	RUNS	WKT	TOTAL	6s	4s	BALLS	NOTES ON DISMISSAL
5:34	2:20	190	1	BOYCOTT	C MARSH	BRIGHT	29	3	89	·	3	136	Edged leg-break to 'keeper when 6 short of Cowdrey's record.
5:34	5:51	17	2	BREARLEY*	LBW	LILLEE	13	1	18	·	2	17	Beaten by short-pitched break that kept low.
5:53	11:59	70	3	GOWER	C BORDER	BRIGHT	23	2	52	·	2	59	2000 RUNS IN TESTS (MIN 5) Edged leg-break via pad to silly point.
12:01	2:37	116	4	GOOCH	BOWLED	BRIGHT	21	4	98	·	3	93	Yorked himself - aiming vast drive.
2:22	4:05	103	5	GATTING	BOWLED	BRIGHT	39	8	167	·	3	71	Missed sweep at leg-break.
2:39	3:02	23	6	WILLEY	BOWLED	BRIGHT	5	5	110	·	1	22	Beaten by flight - played over leg-break - leg stump hit.
3:04	3:19	15	7	BOTHAM	C MARSH	LILLEE	3	6	115	·	·	11	Bottom-edged firm-footed cut.
3:21	3:48	27	8	OLD	C MARSH	ALDERMAN	23	7	154	·	3	24	Edged drive - not in line - away, seamer - low catch.
3:50	(5:42)	92	9	EMBUREY	NOT OUT		37			·	5	79	Missed turn to leg.
4:07	5:37	70	10	TAYLOR	LBW	ALDERMAN	8	9	217	·	·	47	Edged attempted off-drive - high, wide catch.
5:39	5:42	3	11	WILLIS	C MARSH	ALDERMAN	2	10	219	·	·	5	
				EXTRAS	b - lb 6	w 1 nb 9				0	2²	564 balls (inc 12 no balls)	
				TOTAL			219						all out at 5:42 pm 3rd day.

(off 92 overs in 372 min)

14 OVERS 5 BALLS/HOUR
2·38 RUNS/OVER
39 RUNS/100 BALLS

WKT	PARTNERSHIP		RUNS	MINS
1st	Boycott	Brearley	18	17
2nd	Boycott	Gower	34	70
3rd	Boycott	Gooch	37	99
4th	Gooch	Gatting	9	15
5th	Gatting	Willey	12	23
6th	Gatting	Botham	5	15
7th	Gatting	Old	39	27
8th	Gatting	Emburey	13	15
9th	Emburey	Taylor	50	70
10th	Emburey	Willis	2	3
			219	

STUMPS: 49-1 (2ND DAY) (20 BEHIND)
BOYCOTT 9* (60 min) GOWER 20* (41 min)
OFF 13 OVERS IN 60 MIN.

LUNCH: 86-2
BOYCOTT 28* (180 min²) GOOCH 15* (89 min)
OFF 45 OVERS IN 180 MIN.

TEA: 168-8
EMBUREY 2* (21 min) TAYLOR 0* (4 min)
OFF 75 OVERS IN 301 MIN.
LEAD: 99

AUSTRALIA need 151 to win

	RUNS	MINS	OVERS	LAST 50 (in mins)
	50	67	14.5	67
	100	218	54.4	151
	150	272	67.4	54
	200	340	85	68

HRS	OVERS	RUNS
1	13	49
2	17	11
3	15	26
4	15	25
5	15	57
6	15	46

BOWLER	O	M	R	W
LILLEE	26	9	51	2
ALDERMAN	22	5	65	3
HOGG	10	3	19	0
BRIGHT	34	17	68	5
			16	
	92	34	219	10

2ND NEW BALL taken at 5:10 pm 3rd day
- ENGLAND 200-8 after 85 overs

138

AUSTRALIA 2ND INNINGS   REQUIRING 151 RUNS IN A MINIMUM OF 758 MINUTES

IN	OUT	MINS	No.	BATSMAN	HOW OUT	BOWLER	RUNS	WKT	TOTAL	6s	4s	BALLS	NOTES ON DISMISSAL
5.52	12.23	62	1	DYSON	LBW	WILLIS	13	2	19	.	1	46	Played back - late on stroke - ball kept low.
5.52	5.59	7	2	WOOD	LBW	OLD	2	1	2	.	.	5	Beaten by breakback.
6.01	3.40	213	3	BORDER	C' GATTING	EMBUREY	40	5	105	.	4	175	Ground lifting ball from foothold to short square leg.
12.25	12.41	16	4	HUGHES *	C' EMBUREY	WILLIS	5	3	29	.	.	11	Hooked bouncer to long-leg off front foot.
12.43	3.14	114	5	YALLOP	C' BOTHAM	EMBUREY	30	4	87	.	5	96	Edged mid-wicket drive at leg-break to silly-point (wk pad)
3.16	4.24	68	6	KENT	BOWLED	BOTHAM	10	9	121	.	1	45	Yorked - off-driving outside in-swinger.
3.42	3.51	9	7	MARSH †	BOWLED	BOTHAM	4	6	114	.	1	8	Middle stump - drove across line.
3.53	3.54	1	8	BRIGHT	LBW	BOTHAM	0	7	114	.	.	1	1st ball - beaten by sharp breakback.
3.55	4.14	19	9	LILLEE	C' TAYLOR	BOTHAM	3	8	120	.	.	19	Edged firm-footed drive at wide outswinger.
4.16	(4.27)	11	10	HOGG	NOT OUT		0		121	.	.	6	-
4.25	4.27	2	11	ALDERMAN	BOWLED	BOTHAM	0	10	121	.	.	3	Missed drive - bowled leg-stump by inswinger.
				EXTRAS	b1 lb2	w- nb11	14			0	12⁴		

TOTAL   121   all out at 4.27pm on 4th day   415 balls (inc. 13 no balls)

(off 67 overs in 269 minutes)

* CAPTAIN   † WICKET-KEEPER

14 OVERS 5 BALLS/HOUR
1.81 RUNS/OVER
29 RUNS/100 BALLS

BOWLER	O	M	R	W
WILLIS	20	6	37	2
OLD	11	4	19	1
EMBUREY	22	10	40	2
BOTHAM	14	9	11	5
			14	
	67	29	121	10

HRS	OVERS	RUNS	RUNS	MINS	OVERS	LAST 50 (in mins)
1	14	19	50	130	29.3	130
2	13	27	100	218	54.4	88
3	18	23				
4	14	45				

WKT	PARTNERSHIP		RUNS	MINS
1st	Dyson	Wood	2	7
2nd	Dyson	Border	17	53
3rd	Border	Hughes	10	16
4th	Border	Yallop	58	114
5th	Border	Kent	18	24
6th	Kent	Marsh	9	9
7th	Kent	Bright	0	1
8th	Kent	Lillee	6	19
9th	Kent	Hogg	1	8
10th	Hogg	Alderman	0	2
			121	

STUMPS (3RD DAY): 9-1   DYSON 5* (39 min) / BORDER 2* (30 min)
(REQUIRING 142 TO WIN) OFF 9 OVERS IN 39 MIN.

LUNCH: 62-3   BORDER 13* (53 min) / YALLOP 18* (80 min)
(REQUIRING 89 TO WIN) OFF 39 OVERS IN 162 MIN.

ENGLAND won by 29 RUNS
AND TOOK 2-1 LEAD IN SERIES

MAN OF THE MATCH: I.T. BOTHAM
(TOOK 5 WICKETS FOR 1 RUN IN 28 BALLS)
ADJUDICATOR: T.E. BAILEY

TOTAL TIME LOST: NIL

FIFTH TEST   ENGLAND FIRST INNINGS

ENGLAND 1st INNINGS v. AUSTRALIA (5TH TEST) at OLD TRAFFORD, MANCHESTER on AUGUST 13,14,15,16,17, 1981.   TOSS: ENGLAND

IN	OUT	MINS	No.	BATSMAN	HOW OUT	BOWLER	RUNS	WKT	TOTAL	6s	4s	BALLS	NOTES ON DISMISSAL
11:30	11:59	29	1	GOOCH	LBW	LILLEE	10	2	25	·	1	19	Beaten by faster ball.
11:30	11:54	24	2	BOYCOTT	C MARSH	ALDERMAN	10	1	19	·	1	20	Edged via glove & pad low to 'keeper who dived forward.
11:56	6:26	287	3	TAVARÉ	C ALDERMAN	WHITNEY	69	9	175	·	7	193	Edged drive at widish ball to 1st slip.
12:01	2:32	69	4	GOWER	C YALLOP	WHITNEY	23	3	57	·	3	49	Cut to gully. Whitney's 1st Test wicket - 19th ball.
2:34	2:39	5	5	BREARLEY *	LBW	ALDERMAN	2	4	62	·	·	6	Beaten by late movement.
2:41	3:36	55	6	GATTING	C BORDER	LILLEE	32	5	109	·	4	42	Hooked too early at bouncer that 'stopped' - easily to 2nd slip.
3:37	3:38	1	7	BOTHAM	C BRIGHT	LILLEE	0	6	109	·	·	1	Fended lifting ball to gully's left - one-handed catch.
3:40	5:03	63	8	KNOTT †	C BORDER	ALDERMAN	13	7	131	·	1	55	Edged to 2nd slip.
5:05	5:22	17	9	EMBUREY	C BORDER	ALDERMAN	1	8	137	·	·	18	Edged low to 2nd slip. ALDERMAN'S 32nd WKT (SERIES RECORD=E)
5:24	(12:21)	117	10	ALLOTT	NOT OUT		52			1(5)	5	92	Maiden first-class 50 off 92 balls.
6:28	12:21	53	11	WILLIS	C HUGHES	LILLEE	11	10	231	·	1	23	Skied drive to deep extra-cover. LILLEE'S 150th WKT v. ENG.
				EXTRAS	b -	lb 6	w 2	nb -				8	
				TOTAL			231						all out at 12:21 pm on 2nd day.

(OFF 86.1 OVERS IN 368 MIN.)   518 balls (inc 1 no ball)

* CAPTAIN   † WICKET-KEEPER

14 OVERS 0 BALLS/HOUR
2.68 RUNS/OVER
45 RUNS/100 BALLS

WKT	PARTNERSHIP		RUNS	MINS
1st	Gooch	Boycott	19	24
2nd	Gooch	Tavaré	6	3
3rd	Tavaré	Gower	32	69
4th	Tavaré	Brearley	5	5
5th	Tavaré	Gatting	47	55
6th	Tavaré	Botham	0	1
7th	Tavaré	Knott	22	63
8th	Tavaré	Emburey	6	17
9th	Tavaré	Allott	38	62
10th	Allott	Willis	56	53
			231	

RSP at 12:42 pm   LUNCH TAKEN EARLY at 1:15pm

LUNCH: 42-2   TAVARÉ 5* (46 min.)   GOWER 12* (41 min.)
OFF 16.1 OVERS IN 72½ MINUTES

TEA: 119-6   TAVARÉ 26* (71 min.)   KNOTT 10* (30 min.)
OFF 45 OVERS IN 197 MINUTES.

STUMPS: 175-9   ALLOTT 9* (66 min.)   WILLIS 0* (2 min.)
(1st DAY)   OFF 74 OVERS IN 317 MINUTES
43 MINUTES LOST ON FIRST DAY

2nd DAY: ENGLAND ADDED 56 RUNS FOR THEIR LAST WICKET OFF 12.1 OVERS IN 51 MINUTES. - RECORD FOR ENGLAND'S 10TH WKT
*. AUSTRALIA at OLD TRAFFORD (prev 36 BRIGGS/PILLING c.1888)

BOWLER	O	M	R	W
LILLEE	24.1	8	55	4
ALDERMAN	29	5	88	4
WHITNEY	17	3	50	2
BRIGHT	16	6	30	0
			8	
	86.1	22	231	10

2ND NEW BALL TAKEN at 12:10pm on 2nd day - ENGLAND 215-9 after 85 overs.

HRS	OVERS	RUNS
1	14	38
2	12	36
3	14	41
4	16	17
5	15	38
6	13	41

RUNS	MINS	OVERS	LAST 50 (in mins)
50	89	19.3	89
100	158	34.3	69
150	269	63.1	111
200	351	82.2	82

AUSTRALIA 1ST INNINGS   IN REPLY TO ENGLAND'S 231 ALL OUT

IN	OUT	MINS	No.	BATSMAN	HOW OUT	BOWLER	RUNS	WKT	TOTAL	6s	4s	BALLS	NOTES ON DISMISSAL
12·32	12·59	27	1	WOOD	LBW	ALLOTT	19	4	24	1	3	16	Played back and across - hit on back leg.
12·32	12·50	18	2	DYSON	c' BOTHAM	WILLIS	0	1	20	.	.	11	Fended short ball low to 3rd slip. WILLIS'S 100th WKT v.A.
12·52	12·54	2	3	HUGHES *	LBW	WILLIS	4	2	24	.	1	3	Played back to half-volley that came back.
12·55	12·56	1	4	YALLOP	c' BOTHAM	WILLIS	0	3	24	.	.	2	Edged short ball low in front of 3rd slip. WILLIS 3 WKT IN OVER
12·58	2·47	70	5	KENT	c' KNOTT	EMBUREY	52	7	104	.	7	45	Edged square-drive. KNOTT'S 100th DISMISSAL v. AUSTRALIA
1·01	1·31	30	6	BORDER	c' GOWER	BOTHAM	11	5	58	.	1	23	Edged drive at widish off-side ball high to 4th slip.
2·10	2·12	2	7	MARSH †	c' BOTHAM	WILLIS	1	6	59	.	.	2	Edged widish ball to 3rd slip.
2·14	3·39	85	8	BRIGHT	c' KNOTT	BOTHAM	22	10	130	.	2	55	Edged lifting outswinger.
2·49	3·27	38	9	LILLEE	c' GOOCH	BOTHAM	13	8	125	.	2	25	Cubbed half-volley low to square-leg.
3·29	3·35	6	10	WHITNEY	BOWLED	ALLOTT	0	9	126	.	.	7	Hit across leg-stump yorker.
3·57	(3·39)	2	11	ALDERMAN	NOT OUT		2			.	.	1	-

EXTRAS b - lb - w - nb 6 .... 6 ...... 1s 16s ...... 190 balls (inc. 8 no balls)

TOTAL b - lb - w - nb 6 ...... 130 all out at 3·39 pm 2nd day (101 BEHIND)

(OFF 30·2 OVERS IN 148 MINUTES)

* CAPTAIN   † WICKET-KEEPER

HRS	OVERS	RUNS	RUNS	MINS	OVERS	LAST 50 (in mins)
1	12	59	50	52	10	52
2	13	59	100	94	19.1	42

BOWLER	O	M	R	W
WILLIS	14	0	63	4
ALLOTT	6	1	17	2
BOTHAM	6·2	1	28	3
EMBUREY	4	0	16	1
			6	
	30·2	2	13 0	10

WKT	PARTNERSHIP		RUNS	MINS
1st	Wood	Dyson	20	18
2nd	Wood	Hughes	4	2
3rd	Wood	Yallop	0	1
4th	Wood	Kent	0	1
5th	Kent	Border	34	30
6th	Kent	Marsh	1	2
7th	Kent	Bright	45	37
8th	Bright	Lillee	21	38
9th	Bright	Whitney	1	6
10th	Bright	Alderman	4	2

130

12 OVERS 2 BALLS/HOUR
4.29 RUNS/OVER
68 RUNS/100 BALLS

LUNCH: 58-5   KENT 21* (33 min) OFF 11·4 OVERS IN 53 MIN
173 BEHIND

FIFTH TEST   ENGLAND SECOND INNINGS

ENGLAND 2ND INNINGS — 101 RUNS AHEAD ON FIRST INNINGS

IN	OUT	MINS	No.	BATSMAN	HOW OUT	BOWLER	RUNS	WKT	TOTAL	6s	4s	BALLS	NOTES ON DISMISSAL
3-50	4-04	14	1	GOOCH	BOWLED	ALDERMAN	5	1	7	·	1	18	Played across line — bowled leg stump behind legs.
3-50	11-59	170	2	BOYCOTT	LBW	ALDERMAN	37	2	79	·	2	122	Played across straight ball – no movement off seam.
4-06	5-27	423	3	TAVARÉ	C' KENT	ALDERMAN	78	7	282	·	3	289	50 in 306 min. (slowest in English F-C matches) Fended bouncer to 1st slip.
12-01	12-23	22	4	GOWER	C' BRIGHT	LILLEE	1	3	80	·	·	21	Pulled short ball hard to mid-wicket - v. good catch.
12-25	1-28	63	5	GATTING	LBW	ALDERMAN	11	4	98	·	1	43	Beaten by ball that kept low.
1-30	2-26	17	6	BREARLEY *	C' MARSH	ALDERMAN	3	5	104	·	·	20	Alert leg-side catch off leg glance.
2-28	4-51	123	7	BOTHAM	C' MARSH	WHITNEY	118	6	253	6	13	102	Top-edged offside steer. 100 off 86 balls. Most 6s in Test in Eng and v. Aus.
4-53	12-18	115	8	KNOTT	C' DYSON	LILLEE	59	8	356	·	8	89	Cut short ball to deep 3rd man – falling one-handed catch.
5-29	1-40	161	9	EMBUREY	C' KENT	WHITNEY	57	9	396	·	7	122	Edged to 2nd slip - juggling catch. Maiden 50 in Tests.
12-20	1-54	94	10	ALLOTT	C' HUGHES	BRIGHT	14	10	404	·	·	81	Simple catch to mid-off.
1-42	(1-54)	12	11	WILLIS	NOT OUT		5			·	·	6	-
				EXTRAS			16						b 1 lb 12 w - nb 3

TOTAL 404 all out at 1-54 pm 4th day
(OFF 151·4 OVERS ≈ 616 MINUTES)

6s 36 4s 913 balls (inc 3 no balls)

14 OVERS 4 BALLS/HOUR
2·66 RUNS/OVER
44 RUNS/100 BALLS

WKT	PARTNERSHIP		RUNS	MINS
1st	Gooch	Boycott	7	14
2nd	Boycott	Tavaré	72	154
3rd	Tavaré	Gower	1	22
4th	Tavaré	Gatting	18	63
5th	Tavaré	Brearley	6	17
6th	Tavaré	Botham	149	123
7th	Tavaré	Knott	29	34
8th	Knott	Emburey	74	79
9th	Emburey	Allott	40	80
10th	Allott	Willis	8	12
			404	

TEA: 7-1

STUMPS: 70-1 BOYCOTT 0* (20 minutes) TAVARE 0* (4 minutes) OFF 5 OVERS IN 20 MINUTES
(2ND DAY) (1ft AHEAD) BOYCOTT 31* (141 min) TAVARE 29* (125 min) OFF 36 OVERS IN 141 MINUTES

LUNCH: 99-4 TAVARE 38* (247 min) BREARLEY 1* (2 min) OFF 64 OVERS IN 263 MINUTES
(200 AHEAD)

TEA: 226-5 TAVARE 67* (367 min) BOTHAM 94* (103 min) OFF 93 OVERS IN 383 MINUTES
(327 AHEAD)

STUMPS: 345-7 KNOTT 56* (97 min) EMBUREY 27* (61 min) OFF 122 OVERS IN 502 MINUTES
(3RD DAY) (+446)

4TH DAY: ENGLAND ADDED 59 RUNS OFF 29·4 OVERS IN 114 MINUTES.

BOWLER	O	M	R	W
LILLEE	46	13	137	2
ALDERMAN	52	19	109	5
WHITNEY	27	6	74	2
BRIGHT	26·4	12	68	1
			1b	
	151·4	50	404	10

2ND NEW BALL taken at 3-37 pm 3rd day
- ENGLAND 150-5 after 85 overs

HRS	OVERS	RUNS		RUNS	MINS	OVERS	LAST 50 (in mins)
1	15	36		50	94	22.2	94
2	15	25		100	271	66	177
3	15	18		150	346	84.4	75
4	14	12		200	369	89.2	23
5	14	21		250	398	96.4	29
6	14	67		300	457	110.5	59
7	15	82		350	515	125.2	58
8	14	69		400	611	150	96
9	15	40					
10	17	26					

* CAPTAIN † WICKET-KEEPER

AUSTRALIA 2ND INNINGS

FIFTH TEST   AUSTRALIA SECOND INNINGS

REQUIRING 506 RUNS TO WIN IN A MINIMUM OF 605 MINUTES

IN	OUT	MINS	No.	BATSMAN	HOW OUT	BOWLER	RUNS	WKT	TOTAL	6s	4s	BALLS	NOTES ON DISMISSAL
2.35	2.47	12	1	DYSON	RUN OUT (GOWER + GATTING)		5	1	7	.	1	14	Wood refused his call for suicidal run to short extra-cover.
2.35	3.04	29	2	WOOD	c' KNOTT	ALLOTT	6	2	24	.	1	16	Edged swing at widish leg-side long-hop – fine catch.
2.49	4.19	90	3	HUGHES *	LBW	BOTHAM	43	3	119	.	8	72	Played outside line of straight ball – front pad.
3.06	6.21	177	4	YALLOP	BOWLED	EMBUREY	114	4	198	.	17	125	Bowled behind legs by overpitched off-break. (6th Test)
4.21	(4.35)	420	5	BORDER	NOT OUT		123	.	206	.	17	356	Batted throughout with fractured finger (left-hand) (7th in Tests)
6.23	6.46	23	6	KENT	c' BREARLEY	EMBUREY	2	5	206	.	.	17	Pushed to silly-point.
6.48	12.38	110	7	MARSH †	c' KNOTT	WILLIS	47	6	296	1	6	101	Edged drive at off side ball.
12.40	1.57	39	8	BRIGHT	c' KNOTT	WILLIS	5	7	322	.	.	29	Edged or gloved leg glance.
1.59	3.22	83	9	LILLEE	c' BOTHAM	ALLOTT	28	8	373	.	3	65	Edged cut to 2nd slip – superb catch.
3.24	3.37	13	10	ALDERMAN	LBW	BOTHAM	0	9	378	.	.	10	Missed straight ball – front pad.
3.39	4.35	38	11	WHITNEY	c' GATTING	WILLIS	0	10	402	.	.	32	Edged via bad to forward short leg.
				EXTRAS	b – lb 9	w 2 nb 18	29			1⁶	53⁴	837 balls (inc 22 no balls)	

TOTAL (OFF 135.5 OVERS IN 526 MIN)   402 all out at 4.35 pm 5th day.

* CAPTAIN   † WICKET-KEEPER

15 OVERS 3 BALLS/HOUR
2.96 RUNS/OVER
48 RUNS/100 BALLS

BOWLER	O	M	R	W
WILLIS	30.5	2	96	3
ALLOTT	17	3	71	2
BOTHAM	36	16	86	2
EMBUREY	49	9	107	2
GATTING	3	1	13	0
			29	1
	135.5	31	402	10

2ND NEW BALL taken at 12.26 pm 5th day –
AUSTRALIA 291-5 after 85 overs

HRS	OVERS	RUNS
1	12	48
2	16	83
3	15	41
4	15	34
5	16	58
6	16	39
7	15	38
8	17	33

RUNS	MINS	OVERS	LAST 50 (in mins)
50	60	12.2	60
100	84	17.5	24
150	153	37.2	69
200	216	51.5	63
250	282	68.1	66
300	350	87.1	68
350	426	107.3	76
400	522	134.4	96

TEA: 133-3   373 REQUIRED
   YALLOP 67* (96 min.) BORDER 5* (21 min.) off 30 overs in 127 MIN.

STUMPS: 210-5 (4TH DAY) (296 REQ'D)
   BORDER 28* (141 min.) MARSH 2* (12 min.) off 60 overs in 247 MIN

LUNCH: 317-6   189 REQUIRED
   BORDER 70* (263 min.) BRIGHT 2* (22 min.) off 92 overs in 369 MIN.

TEA: 398-9   108 REQUIRED
   BORDER 119* (414 min.) WHITNEY 0* (32 min.) off 134 overs in 526 MIN

ENGLAND won by 103 runs to take 3-1 lead in series and to retain the Ashes. (TOTAL TIME LOST 43 min.)
MAN OF THE MATCH: I.T. BOTHAM

WKT	PARTNERSHIP		RUNS	MINS
1st	Dyson	Wood	7	12
2nd	Wood	Hughes	17	15
3rd	Hughes	Yallop	95	73
4th	Yallop	Border	79	102
5th	Border	Kent	8	23
6th	Border	Marsh	90	110
7th	Border	Bright	26	39
8th	Border	Lillee	51	83
9th	Border	Alderman	5	13
10th	Border	Whitney	24	38
			402	

SIXTH TEST   AUSTRALIA FIRST INNINGS

AUSTRALIA 1ST INNINGS v ENGLAND (6TH TEST) at KENNINGTON OVAL, LONDON, on AUGUST 27, 28, 29, 31, SEPTEMBER 1, 1981.

TOSS: ENGLAND — BREARLEY'S 50TH CATCH IN TESTS.

IN	OUT	MINS	No.	BATSMAN	HOW OUT	BOWLER	RUNS	WKT	TOTAL	6s	4s	BALLS	NOTES ON DISMISSAL
11:00	2:27	168	1	WOOD	c BREARLEY	BOTHAM	66	1	120	-	6	129	Changed mind in mid-hook at bouncer – skier behind sticks
11:00	2:38	179	2	KENT	c GATTING	BOTHAM	54	2	125	-	7	129	Mistimed off-drive – simple catch to mid-off. (100 RUNS v ENGLAND, 200 RUNS in TESTS)
2:29	4:31	101	3	HUGHES *	HIT WICKET	BOTHAM	31	4	199	-	1	67	Left leg hit stump when completing pull to mid-wkt.
2:40	3:39	59	4	YALLOP	c BOTHAM	WILLIS	26	3	169	-	1	50	Edged to 3rd slip – fast, high, right-handed catch.
4:01 (2:29)	(2:29)	290	5	BORDER	NOT OUT		106			-	13	230	(8th in Tests – second in successive innings – both not out.
4:33	11:23	112	6	WELLHAM	BOWLED	WILLIS	24	5	260	-	1	93	Late on fast ball which came through gate to hit middle & off.
11:25	11:43	18	7	MARSH †	c BOTHAM	WILLIS	12	6	280	-	2	18	Edged tentative push to 3rd slip via 2nd slip (Tavare).
11:45	12:26	41	8	BRIGHT	c BREARLEY	BOTHAM	11	7	303	-	1	30	Edged drive at outswinging half-volley low to 1st slip.
12:28	1:45	36	9	LILLEE	BOWLED	WILLIS	11	8	319	-	1	36	Beaten by pace – through 'gate'. WILLIS 110 wkts v AUS (RECORD)
1:47	1:49	2	10	ALDERMAN	BOWLED	BOTHAM	0	9	320	-	-	2	Beaten by late inswinger.
1:51	1:59	38	11	WHITNEY	BOWLED	BOTHAM	4	10	352	-	1	13	Missed straight ball. WHITNEY'S FIRST RUNS IN TEST, AND HIGHEST SCORE (* = FIRST BOUNDARY) IN FIRST-CLASS CRICKET.
				EXTRAS	b4 lb 6	w1 nb4	15			0	33*	(inc 5 no balls)	
				TOTAL			352					797 balls	all out at 2:29 pm on 2nd day.

(OFF 132 OVERS IN 531 MINUTES)

* CAPTAIN   † WICKET-KEEPER

WKT	PARTNERSHIP		RUNS	MINS
1st	Wood	Kent	120	168
2nd	Kent	Hughes	5	9
3rd	Hughes	Yallop	44	59
4th	Hughes	Border	30	30
5th	Border	Wellham	61	112
6th	Border	Marsh	20	18
7th	Border	Bright	23	41
8th	Border	Lillee	16	36
9th	Border	Alderman	1	2
10th	Border	Whitney	32	38
			352	

14 OVERS 5 BALLS/HOUR
2.67 RUNS/OVER
44 RUNS/100 BALLS

LUNCH: 85–0   WOOD 50* KENT 34*   OFF 31 OVERS IN 122 MIN.

TEA: 169–3   HUGHES 21* (70 min)   OFF 58.5 OVERS IN 241 MIN.

STUMPS: 251–4 (1ST DAY)   BORDER 51* (122 min) WELLHAM 19* (89 min)   OFF 91 OVERS IN 363 MINUTES

LUNCH: 318–7   BORDER 79* (242 min) LILLEE 11* (32 min)   OFF 120 OVERS IN 483 MINUTES

AUSTRALIA'S FIRST 100 RUNS FIRST-WICKET PARTNERSHIP SINCE 1ST JANUARY 1977, AND THEIR 50TH CENTURY OPENING STAND IN ALL TESTS.

HRS	OVERS	RUNS
1	15	46
2	15	38
3	14	41
4	15	44
5	15	41
6	16	40
7	14	39
8	15	29

RUNS	MINS	OVERS	LAST 50 (in mins)
50	67	16	67
100	138	35	71
150	213	52	75
200	275	67	62
250	357	89.3	82
300	440	108.5	83
350	527	131.1	87

BOWLER	O	M	R	W
WILLIS	31	6	91	4
HENDRICK	31	8	63	0
BOTHAM	47	13	125	6
EMBUREY	23	2	58	0
			15	
	132	29	352	10

2ND NEW BALL TAKEN at 6-148 mins on 1st day –
AUSTRALIA 247-4 after 87-2 overs.
BOTHAM 5 wkts in a Test innings 17 times (41 Tests)

ENGLAND 1ST INNINGS

IN REPLY TO AUSTRALIA'S 352 ALL OUT

IN	OUT	MINS	No.	BATSMAN	HOW OUT	BOWLER	RUNS	WKT	TOTAL	6s	4s	BALLS	NOTES ON DISMISSAL
2.41	4.20	441	1	BOYCOTT	C YALLOP	LILLEE	137	7	293	·	7	321	Edged low to gully's right - superb diving catch
2.41	4.34	93	2	LARKINS	C ALDERMAN	LILLEE	34	1	61	·	4	75	Edged off-glide to 2nd slip. LARKINS' HS in TESTS. (21st in TESTS (7th × INNS. (24th F.c.
4.35	11.42	127	3	TAVARÉ	C MARSH	LILLEE	24	2	131	·	2	91	Under-edged square cut.
11.44	3.00	157	4	GATTING	BOWLED	LILLEE	53	3	246	·	5	114	Played no stroke to straight ball on off stump. (FIRST BALL WITH NEW BALL)
3.02	3.07	5	5	BREARLEY *	C BRIGHT	ALDERMAN	0	4	248	·	·	6	Edged (but shoulder) lifting ball to 3rd slip.
3.09	3.11	2	6	PARKER	C KENT	ALDERMAN	0	5	248	·	·	3	Followed outswinger - edged to 2nd slip.
3.12	3.23	11	7	BOTHAM	C YALLOP	LILLEE	3	6	256	·	·	5	Edged to 2nd gully.
3.25	4.52	68	8	KNOTT †	BOWLED	LILLEE	36	10	314	·	4	49	Leg stump - missed pull.
4.22	4.23	1	9	EMBUREY	LBW	LILLEE	0	8	293	·	·	2	Pushed forward — beaten by breakback.
4.25	4.38	13	10	WILLIS	BOWLED	ALDERMAN	3	9	302	·	·	7	Played no stroke to breakback that hit off stump.
4.39	(4.52)	13	11	HENDRICK	NOT OUT		0			·	·	6	-

EXTRAS   b - lb 9   24   0⁴ 22⁴ 679 balls (inc 15 no balls)

b - lb 9 w 3 nb 12

TOTAL (OFF 110.4 OVERS IN 472 MIN)   314 all out   (38 RUNS BEHIND)

* CAPTAIN † WICKET-KEEPER

14 OVERS 0 BALLS/HOUR
2.84 RUNS/OVER
46 RUNS/100 BALLS

BOWLER	O	M	R	W
LILLEE	31.4	4	89	7
ALDERMAN	35	4	84	3
WHITNEY	23	3	76	0
BRIGHT	21	6	41	0
			24	
	110.4	17	314	10

2nd NEW BALL taken at 3:00 pm on 3rd day - ENGLAND 246-2 after 90 overs.

HRS	OVERS	RUNS
1	13	29
2	15	45
3	15	26
4	15	36
5	13	40
6	15	52
7	13	46

RUNS	MINS	OVERS	LAST 50 (in mins)
50	84	18.4	84
100	179	42.5	95
150	262	62.3	83
200	322	76.2	60
250	394	92.4	72
300	453	106.1	59

TEA: 29-0   BOYCOTT 13* OFF 13 OVERS   LARKINS 14*   59 MIN.

STUMPS: 100-1 (2nd DAY) (252 BEHIND)   BOYCOTT 47* (179 MIN)   TAVARE 8* (35 MIN)   OFF 43 OVERS IN 179 MIN.

LUNCH: 176-2 (176 BEHIND)   BOYCOTT 87* (299 MIN)   GATTING 16* (76 MIN)   OFF 71 OVERS IN 299 MIN.

TEA: 275-6 (77 BEHIND)   BOYCOTT 135* (421 MIN)   KNOTT 4* (17 MIN)   OFF 93 OVERS IN 421 MIN.

LILLEE'S BEST ANALYSIS IN TESTS (PREV 6-26) AND THE 19th TIME HE HAS TAKEN FIVE OR MORE WICKETS IN A TEST MATCH INNINGS.

WKT	PARTNERSHIP		RUNS	MINS
1st	Boycott	Larkins	61	93
2nd	Boycott	Tavaré	70	127
3rd	Boycott	Gatting	115	157
4th	Boycott	Brearley	2	5
5th	Boycott	Parker	0	2
6th	Boycott	Botham	8	11
7th	Boycott	Knott	37	36
8th	Knott	Emburey	0	1
9th	Knott	Willis	9	13
10th	Knott	Hendrick	12	13

314

AUSTRALIA 2ND INNINGS   38 RUNS AHEAD ON FIRST INNINGS

SIXTH TEST   AUSTRALIA SECOND INNINGS

IN	OUT	MINS	No.	BATSMAN	HOW OUT	BOWLER	RUNS	WKT	TOTAL	6s	4s	BALLS	NOTES ON DISMISSAL
5.04	11.05	62	1	WOOD	C' KNOTT	HENDRICK	21	3	41	.	1	46	Pushed forward - edged away, seamer high to Knott left. [KNOTT'S 250th TEST MATCH CATCH]
5.04	5.37	33	2	KENT	C' BREARLEY	BOTHAM	7	1	26	.	1	17	Edged outswinger to 1st slip.
5.39	6.01	22	3	HUGHES*	LBW	HENDRICK	6	2	36	.	1	24	Beaten by breakback in last over of 3rd day.
11.00	12.25	85	4	YALLOP	BOWLED	HENDRICK	35	4	104	.	3	62	Played on (inside edge) - cutting at offside ball.
11.07	2.59	192	5	BORDER	C' TAVARÉ	EMBUREY	84	5	205	.	8	152	Edged leg-break to 1st slip.
12.27	5.53	266	6	WELLHAM	LBW	BOTHAM	103	8	343	.	12	221	HUNDRED ON DEBUT. Missed breakback that kept low. [24 minutes] on 99
3.01	4.58	96	7	MARSH†	C' GATTING	BOTHAM	52	6	291	.	7	83	3000 RUNS IN TESTS. Miscued hook to mid-wkt. BOTHAM'S 20th TEST WKT.
5.02	5.32	30	8	BRIGHT	BOWLED	BOTHAM	11	7	332	.	2	14	Drove across straight ball.
5.34	(5.59)	25	9	LILLEE	NOT OUT		8			.	1	12	
5.55	5.59	4	10	WHITNEY	C' BOTHAM	HENDRICK	0	9	344	.	.	3	Edged to 3rd slip.
			11	ALDERMAN	Did not bat								
				EXTRAS	b 1 lb 8 w 1 nb 7		17			0	36	634 balls (inc 8 no balls)	

TOTAL (OFF 104.2 OVERS IN 416 MIN) **344-9 DECLARED** before start of 5th day

* CAPTAIN   † WICKET-KEEPER

BOWLER	O	M	R	W
WILLIS	10	0	41	0
BOTHAM	42	9	128	4
HENDRICK	29.2	6	82	4
EMBUREY	23	3	76	1
			17	
	104.2	18	344	9

2ND NEW BALL TAKEN at 4.32pm on 4th day
- AUSTRALIA 266-5 after 85 overs.

HRS	OVERS	RUNS
1	15	41
2	13	55
3	17	40
4	16	49
5	16	48
6	15	58

RUNS	MINS	OVERS	LAST 50 (in mins)
50	77	18.5	77
100	124	28.4	47
150	182	47.1	58
200	254	63.5	72
250	314	81	60
300	370	94.4	56

STUMPS: 36-2 (3RD DAY) (7+ LEAD)

LUNCH: 132-4   LEAD: 170

TEA: 232-5   LEAD: 270

STUMPS 344-9 (4TH DAY)   AUSTRALIA 382 AHEAD

WOOD 20*
OFF 13.4 OVERS IN 57 MIN
BORDER 34* (113 MIN)
WELLHAM 19* (33 MIN)
OFF 44.4 OVERS IN 177 MIN
WELLHAM 68* (153 MIN)
MARSH 15* (39 MIN)
OFF 76 OVERS IN 297 MIN
LILLEE 8* (25 MIN)
OFF 104.2 OVERS IN 416 MIN
AUSTRALIA 382 AHEAD

ENGLAND set to score 383 RUNS in a maximum of 360 MINUTES

15 OVERS 0 BALLS/HOUR
3.30 RUNS/OVER
54 RUNS/100 BALLS

WKT	PARTNERSHIP		RUNS	MINS
1st	Wood	Kent	26	33
2nd	Wood	Hughes	10	22
3rd	Wood	Yallop	5	5
4th	Yallop	Border	63	78
5th	Border	Wellham	101	112
6th	Wellham	Marsh	86	96
7th	Wellham	Bright	41	30
8th	Wellham	Lillee	11	19
9th	Lillee	Whitney	1	4
10th				344

ENGLAND 2ND INNINGS   REQUIRING 383 RUNS IN A MINIMUM OF 360 MINUTES

IN	OUT	MINS	No.	BATSMAN	HOW OUT	BOWLER	RUNS	WKT	TOTAL	6s	4s	BALLS	NOTES ON DISMISSAL
10·30	10·32	2	1	BOYCOTT	LBW	LILLEE	0	1	0	·	·	4	Pushed forward to quicker, shortish ball that kept low.
10·30	1·20	119	2	LARKINS	c ALDERMAN	LILLEE	24	3	88	·	4	78	Sharply lifting ball hit bat shoulder – held at 2nd slip.
10·34	11·18	44	3	TAVARÉ	c KENT	WHITNEY	8	2	18	·	·	36	Followed ball angled across him – edged to 1st slip.
11·20	1·36	85	4	GATTING	c KENT	LILLEE	56	4	101	·	7	70	Edged sharply lifting ball to 1st slip.
1·22	2·17	55	5	PARKER	c KENT	ALDERMAN	13	5	127	·	2	46	Edged defensive push low to 1st slip.
1·38	5·01	166	6	BREARLEY *	c MARSH	LILLEE	51	7	237	·	7	160	Edged ball that lifted and left him.
2·19	2·29	10	7	BOTHAM	LBW	ALDERMAN	16	6	144	·	2	14	Missed pull at ball on middle and leg stumps. ALDERMAN 42nd wkt of series
2·31	(5·55)	167	8	KNOTT †	NOT OUT		70			·	11	138	
5·03	(5·55)	52	9	EMBUREY	NOT OUT		5			·	·	33	
			10	WILLIS	Did not bat								
			11	HENDRICK									
				EXTRAS	b 2 lb 5 w 2 nb 9		18						0^6 33^4 579 balls (inc 9 no balls)
				TOTAL	(OFF 95 OVERS IN 357 MINUTES)		261-7						

* CAPTAIN   † WICKET-KEEPER

16 OVERS 0 BALLS/HOUR
2·75 RUNS/OVER
45 RUNS/100 BALLS

WKT	PARTNERSHIP		RUNS	MINS
1st	Boycott	Larkins	0	2
2nd	Larkins	Tavaré	18	44
3rd	Larkins	Gatting	70	69
4th	Gatting	Parker	13	14
5th	Parker	Brearley	26	39
6th	Brearley	Botham	17	10
7th	Brearley	Knott	93	113
8th	Knott	Embury	24*	52
			261	

LUNCH: 83-2 [11 MINUTES LOST (BAD LIGHT) 11·58-12·09]
(REQUIRING 300 RUNS in 240)
LARKINS 22* (105 min)
GATTING 46* (59min, 46b)
OFF 25 OVERS IN 109 MIN

TEA: 178-6
BUSP at 3·09 (1 wicket early)
BREARLEY 27* (91 MIN)
KNOTT 19* (38 MIN)
OFF 58 OVERS IN 228 MIN

MATCH DRAWN – 20 overs ended at 5·55pm
ENGLAND WON SERIES 3–1 (2 DRAWN)
BREARLEY UNDEFEATED AS CAPTAIN IN 19 HOME TESTS

MAN OF THE MATCH: D.K. LILLEE
(Adjudicator: F.W. Bennett)
MAN OF THE SERIES: I.T. BOTHAM
(Adjudicator: A.V. Bedser)

TOTAL TIME LOST IN MATCH: 27 MINUTES

BOWLER	O	M	R	W
LILLEE	30	10	70	4
ALDERMAN	19	6	60	2
WHITNEY	11	4	46	1
BRIGHT	27	12	50	0
YALLOP	8	2	17	0
			18	
	95	34	261	7

2ND NEW BALL taken at 5·14 pm 5th day
- ENGLAND 246-7 after 85 overs (10 overs left)

HRS	OVERS	RUNS
1	14	27
2	14	61
3	17	42
4	17	63
5	20	44

RUNS	MINS	OVERS	LAST 50 (in mins)
50	85	19.4	85
100	130	31	45
150	203	50.4	73
200	255	67.3	52
250	320	86	65

TEST MATCH SUMMARY

ENGLAND - BATTING

Name	M	I	NO	HS	Runs	Avge	100	50	6s	4s	Minutes	Balls	Runs/100 balls
A.P.E. KNOTT	2	4	1	70*	178	59.33	-	2	-	24	413	331	54
C.J. TAVARÉ	2	4	0	78	179	44.75	-	2	-	12	881	609	29
G.R. DILLEY	3	6	2	56	150	37.50	-	1	-	23	274	218	69
I.T. BOTHAM	6	12	1	149*	399	36.27	2	1	7	57	609	428	93
G. BOYCOTT	6	12	0	137	392	32.66	1	1	-	22	1650	1179	33
M.W. GATTING	6	12	0	59	370	30.83	-	4	1	41	1032	757	49
J.E. EMBUREY	4	7	2	57	134	26.80	-	1	-	13	533	411	33
D.I. GOWER	5	10	0	89	250	25.00	-	1	1	31	816	615	41
P. WILLEY	4	8	0	82	179	22.37	-	1	1	25	542	409	44
C.M. OLD	2	4	1	29	63	21.00	-	-	-	9	120	82	77
J.M. BREARLEY	4	8	0	51	141	17.62	-	1	-	18	473	400	35
G.A. GOOCH	5	10	0	44	139	13.90	-	-	-	19	370	295	47
R.A. WOOLMER	2	4	0	21	30	7.50	-	-	-	5	175	133	23
M. HENDRICK	2	3	3	6*	6	-	-	-	-	1	37	16	38
R.G.D. WILLIS	6	10	2	13	43	5.37	-	-	-	4	169	84	51
R.W. TAYLOR	3	6	0	9	23	3.83	-	-	1	1	136	102	23
Also batted:-													
P.J.W. ALLOTT	1	2	1	52*	66	66.00	-	1	-	5†	211	173	38
W. LARKINS	1	2	0	34	58	29.00	-	-	-	8	212	153	38
P.W.G. PARKER	1	2	0	13	13	6.50	-	-	-	2	57	49	27
P.R. DOWNTON	1	2	0	8	11	5.50	-	-	-	-	54	35	31
Totals	66	128	13	(149*)	2824	24.55	3	16	11	320	8764	6479	44

* not out   † plus one 'five'

AUSTRALIA - BATTING

Name	M	I	NO	HS	Runs	Avge	100	50	6s	4s	Minutes	Balls	Runs/100 balls
A.R. BORDER	6	12	3	123*	533	59·22	2	3	1	62	1799	1451	37
M.F. KENT	3	6	0	54	171	28·50	-	2	-	22	482	334	51
G.M. WOOD	6	12	1	66	310	28·18	-	2	1	31	808	636	49
G.N. YALLOP	6	12	0	114	316	26·33	1	1	-	34	892	695	45
K.J. HUGHES	6	12	0	89	300	25·00	-	1	-	35	885	713	42
D.K. LILLEE	6	10	3	40*	153	21·85	-	-	-	19	435	355	43
J. DYSON	5	10	0	102	206	20·60	1	-	-	20	795	569	36
R.W. MARSH	6	11	0	52	216	19·63	-	1	1	33	509	426	51
T.M. CHAPPELL	3	6	1	27	79	15·80	-	-	-	3	528	418	19
R.J. BRIGHT	5	9	0	33	127	14·11	-	-	-	15	482	345	37
G.F. LAWSON	3	5	1	14	38	9·50	-	-	-	5	123	88	43
T.M. ALDERMAN	6	9	5	12*	22	5·50	-	-	-	1	139	97	23
M.R. WHITNEY	2	4	0	4	4	1·00	-	-	-	1	86	55	7
R.M. HOGG	2	3	1	0*	0	0·00	-	-	-	-	22	13	0
Also batted :-													
D.M. WELLHAM	1	2	0	103	127	63·50	1	-	-	13	378	314	40
Totals	66	123	15	(123*)	2602	24·09	5	10	3	294	8363	6509	40

* not out

COMPARATIVE SCORING RATES

ENGLAND   46·8 RUNS PER 100 BALLS (3034 RUNS, INC. 210 EXTRAS, OFF 6479 BALLS)
AUSTRALIA   44·0 RUNS PER 100 BALLS (2865 RUNS, INC. 263 EXTRAS, OFF 6509 BALLS)

ENGLAND - BOWLING

Name	O	M	R	W	Avge	BB	5w	10w	Balls/wicket	Runs/100 balls	No balls	Wides
G.R.DILLEY	98	24	275	14	19·64	4/24	-	-	42	47	22	7
I.T.BOTHAM	272·3	81	700	34	20·58	6/95	3	1	48	43	2	8
R.G.D.WILLIS	252·4	56	666	29	22·96	8/43	1	-	52	44	138	-
J.E.EMBUREY	193·5	58	399	12	33·25	4/43	-	-	97	34	2	-
C.M.OLD	84	27	175	5	35·00	3/44	-	-	101	35	5	-
M.HENDRICK	100·2	28	221	6	36·83	4/82	-	-	100	37	-	1
Also bowled:-												
P.J.W.ALLOTT	23	4	88	4	22·00	2/17	-	-	35	64	-	-
P.WILLEY	16	3	35	1	35·00	1/31	-	-	96	36	-	-
G.BOYCOTT	3	2	2	0	-	-	-	-	-	11	-	-
M.W.GATTING	3	1	13	0	-	-	-	-	-	72	2	-
G.A.GOOCH	10	4	28	0	-	-	-	-	-	47	-	-
Totals	1056·2	288	2602	105	24·78	(8/43)	4	1	60	41	171	16

ENGLAND - FIELDING (58 caught, 0 stumped)

13 - TAYLOR. 12 - BOTHAM. 8 - GATTING. 6 - KNOTT.
4 - BREARLEY. 3 - GOWER. 2 - BOYCOTT, DOWNTON, WILLIS,
WOOLMER. 1 - DILLEY, EMBUREY, GOOCH, TAVARÉ.

150

AUSTRALIA - BOWLING

Name	O	M	R	W	Avge	BB	5w	10w	Balls/ wicket	Runs/ 100 balls	No balls	Wides
T.M.ALDERMAN	325	76	893	42	21.26	6/135	4	-	46	46	58	5
D.K.LILLEE	311.4	81	870	39	22.30	7/89	2	1	48	47	11	12
G.F.LAWSON	106.1	30	285	12	23.75	7/81	1	-	53	45	13	5
R.J.BRIGHT	191.4	82	390	12	32.50	5/68	1	-	96	34	1	-
M.R.WHITNEY	78	16	246	5	49.20	2/50	-	-	94	53	-	-
Also bowled:-												
R.M.HOGG	40.4	8	123	4	30.75	3/47	-	-	61	50	29	-
G.N.YALLOP	8	2	17	0	-	-	-	-	-	35	-	-
Totals	1061.1	295	2824	114	24.77	(7/81)	8	1	56	44	112	22

AUSTRALIA - FIELDING (74 caught, 0 stumped)

23 - MARSH. 12 - BORDER. 8 - ALDERMAN. 7 - YALLOP.
6 - KENT. 4 - BRIGHT, WOOD. 3 - HUGHES. 2 - CHAPPELL.
DYSON. 1 - HOGG, LILLEE, substitute.

COMPARATIVE BOWLING RATES

ENGLAND   14 OVERS 5 BALLS PER HOUR (1056.2 OVERS IN 4273 MINUTES)
AUSTRALIA 14 OVERS 1 BALL PER HOUR   (1061.1 OVERS IN 4483 MINUTES)

TEST CAREER RECORDS – ENGLAND

Name	Age†	M	I	NO	HS	Runs	Avge	100	50	Ct	St	Balls	R	W	Avge	BB	5w	10w
P.J.W.ALLOTT	24	1	2	1	52*	66	66.00	-	1	-	-	138	88	4	22.00	2/17	-	-
I.T.BOTHAM	25	41	64	3	149*	1977	32.40	8	5	55	-	9709	4284	202	21.20	8/34	17	4
G.BOYCOTT	40	104	185	22	246*	7802	47.86	21	40	31	-	944	382	7	54.57	3/47	-	-
J.M.BREARLEY	39	39	66	3	91	1442	22.88	-	9	52	-	-						
G.R.DILLEY	22	12	20	7	56	243	18.69	-	1	3	-	2134	1051	38	27.65	4/24	1	-
P.R.DOWNTON	24	4	7	1	26*	59	9.83	-	-	8	-	-						
J.E.EMBUREY	29	18	28	6	57	322	14.63	-	1	13	-	4123	1386	44	31.50	5/124	1	-
M.W.GATTING	24	14	26	1	59	618	24.72	-	6	14	-	26	14	0	-	-	-	-
G.A.GOOCH	28	35	63	3	153	2000	33.33	3	11	31	-	738	271	6	45.16	2/16	-	-
D.I.GOWER	24	31	53	4	200*	2042	41.67	4	8	15	-	-						
M.HENDRICK	32	30	35	15	15	128	6.40	-	-	25	-	6208	2248	87	25.83	4/28	-	-
A.P.E.KNOTT	35	95	149	15	135	4389	32.75	5	30	250	19	-						
W.LARKINS	27	6	11	0	34	176	16.00	-	-	3	-	-						
C.M.OLD	32	46	66	9	65	845	14.82	-	2	22	-	8858	4020	143	28.11	7/50	4	-
P.W.G.PARKER	25	1	2	0	13	13	6.50	-	-	3	-	-						
C.J.TAVARÉ	26	4	8	0	78	244	30.50	-	2	3	-	-						
R.W.TAYLOR	40	29	39	3	97	643	17.86	-	2	92	6	-						
P.WILLEY	31	20	38	5	102*	923	27.96	2	4	3	-	1067	441	6	73.50	2/73	-	-
R.G.D.WILLIS	32	63	90	40	24*	555	11.10	-	-	24	-	12387	5709	227	25.14	8/43	13	-
R.A.WOOLMER	33	19	34	2	149	1059	33.09	3	2	10	-	546	299	4	74.75	1/8	-	-

* not out   † age at end of series (1st September 1981)

152

TEST CAREER RECORDS – AUSTRALIA

Name	Age†	M	I	NO	HS	Runs	Avge	100	50	Ct	St		Balls	R	W	Avge	BB	5w	10w
T.M.ALDERMAN	25	6	9	5	12*	22	5·50	-	-	8	-		1950	893	42	21·26	6/135	4	-
A.R.BORDER	26	33	61	11	162	2593	51·86	8	14	41	-		938	298	8	37·25	2/35	-	-
R.J.BRIGHT	27	14	23	4	33	269	14·15	-	-	7	-		3106	1126	34	33·11	7/87	3	1
T.M.CHAPPELL	28	3	6	1	27	79	15·80	-	-	2	-		-						
J.DYSON	27	14	27	2	102	520	20·80	1	1	3	-		-						
R.M.HOGG	30	22	36	4	36	246	7·68	-	-	5	-		4652	1937	82	23·62	6/74	5	2
K.J.HUGHES	27	39	72	4	213	2673	39·30	5	14	31	-		66	20	0	-	-	-	-
M.F.KENT	27	3	6	0	54	171	28·50	-	2	6	-		-						
G.F.LAWSON	23	4	6	1	16	54	10·80	-	-	-	-		757	350	15	23·33	7/81	1	-
D.K.LILLEE	32	54	72	20	73*	804	15·46	-	1	14	-		14648	6736	290	23·22	7/89	19	6
R.W.MARSH	33	74	118	11	132	3044	28·44	3	15	265	11		60	51	0	-	-	-	-
D.M.WELLHAM	22	1	2	0	103	127	63·50	1	-	-	-		-						
M.R.WHITNEY	22	2	4	0	4	4	1·00	-	-	-	-		468	246	5	49·20	2/50	-	-
G.M.WOOD	24	28	55	3	126	1704	32·76	5	7	25	-		-						
G.N.YALLOP	28	31	59	3	172	2043	36·48	6	7	16	-		192	116	1	116·00	1/21	-	-

* not out   † age at end of series (1st September 1981)

KIRKSTALL LANE END

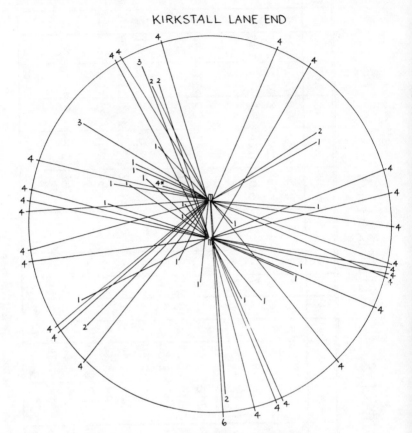

MAIN STAND END

Runs	Balls	Minutes	6s	4s
50	57	110	-	8
100	87	155	1	19
149	148	219	1	27

Bowler	Balls	Runs	6s	4s
ALDERMAN	62	68	1	11
BRIGHT	21	15	-	3
LAWSON	44	44	-	8
LILLEE	21	22	-	5

BOTHAM'S SCORING SEQUENCE

000204200004010000100041000000031
0013014204*00100040400000040404400
444104000000640100040404†400010201
0001000100010040001000401042041 00
401000441 00040000000.

* 4 overthrows to the mid-wicket boundary
† off a no-ball

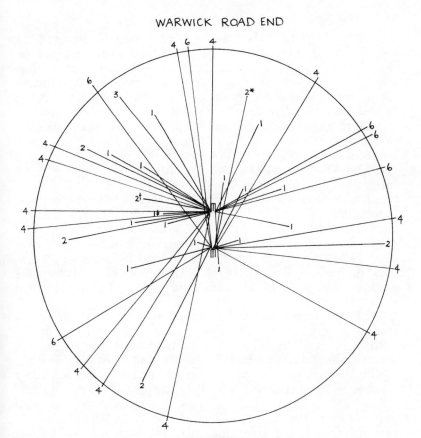

WARWICK ROAD END

STRETFORD END

Runs	Balls	Minutes	6ˢ	4ˢ
50	60	76	2	6
100	86	104	5	11
118	102	123	6	13

Bowler	Balls	Runs	6ˢ	4ˢ
ALDERMAN	17	24	1	3
BRIGHT	36	25	2	2
LILLEE	24	45	3	4
WHITNEY	25	24	-	4

BOTHAM'S SCORING SEQUENCE

00000011000100000000000000000000
110441041001010000004212̈42*161642†
24041‡460020000406004300260000
10601400400 W.

N new ball taken at 3·37 pm (Botham 28 off 53 balls)

* dropped by WHITNEY at deep mid-off (off ALDERMAN)

† including one overthrow

‡ overthrow

W caught by MARSH off WHITNEY

Epilogue

After the catastrophic upheaval suffered by cricket at the hands of the Packer organization four years ago what the game needed, more almost than anything, was a memorable series between the two ancient rivals, England and Australia. "Memorable", of course, is too mild a word to describe the happenings of the few crowded weeks wherein what had seemed an absolutely assured retention of The Ashes by Australia was dissolved, chiefly by the feats of Ian Botham, whose performances at Headingley, Edgbaston and Old Trafford will become an unforgettable legend in the history of cricket.

It has been said with truth that in terms of batting technique especially these are, by Test reckoning, ordinary sides. Equally truly it must be added that followers at large do not aspire to judge the more refined skills of the game; nor have they ever done. They may apprehend instinctively the genius of a few great players – the artistry of a Compton or a Harvey for instance, or, to extend the field of view, of a Sobers or a Richards.

What supporters of cricket expect is positive action and a contest waged within the confines of sportsmanship. If the exchanges are close and exciting so much the better. If a match contains, in addition, wholly unexpected shifts of fortune it has all the ingredients that go to give our ancient game so deep a fascination for such a wide variety of people.

My job is to try to put this series fairly briefly into historical perspective rather than to add to the analytical impressions of my old friend and colleague, Michael Melford. So I must confine myself to underlining two axioms sometimes either ignored or disputed which surely are part of the essence of cricket.

In this age of deep critical investigation it is apt to be forgotten that cricket is confounding expectation all the time. Occasionally this propensity altogether exceeds the bounds of reason, as happened at Headingley when England's chances were rated (foolishly) at 500 to 1. Fowler's Match, brought in aptly enough as an epic equally incredible, is a famous example from schoolboy cricket still quoted more than half a century later.

Every cricketer can recall occasions in his own experience the facts of which are only slightly less difficult to credit. Yet the first-class players of today are often quoted knowingly in advance as saying that this or that will be "a 300 wicket" or "a 150 wicket" as the case may be. What is more, they do their best to make the play conform to their prognosis, adjusting their tactics accordingly: which is one reason, perhaps why three-day county cricket no longer exerts quite its old appeal.

My second point relates to the importance of captaincy. In no games perhaps is the subtle handling of men and the exercise of tactics more important than in cricket. Yet many dismiss the influence of leadership. Well, those who have maintained that it counts for little have a tough case to argue in the light of Botham's contrasts of fortune before his elevation to the captaincy, during it, and after he had been relieved of it. Directly Mike Brearley returned to the side it wore a different look almost at once, while Botham, relieved of a burden to which he had no training and, as it turned out, small aptitude, and to which he should never have been subjected, forthwith resumed the match-winning mantle of hitherto.

I firmly believe that for various reasons, including, of course, the much higher financial rewards now attaching to success, intelligent, firm, sympathetic leadership in the professional game is more important than it ever was.

Be that as it may, how stands 1981 in the long procession of Anglo-Australian Test matches which began just over a century ago at Melbourne on what Keith Dunstan has aptly called "The paddock that grew"? As has been noted already the 1894/5 series in Australia was a marvellously exciting one: it was also the first played in Australia which – thanks to the *Pall Mall Gazette* who arranged for a full cable service to catch their afternoon editions – really captured the interest of the English public at home.

The next two decades (known by historians as "The Golden Age of Cricket") saw this interest expand, series by series, both in England and abroad. There was the great series of 1902, fought out by two of the strongest sides ever to contest The Ashes which will be ever remembered for Jessop's 104 in 75 minutes on a turning Oval pitch which enabled England to score 263 to win after half the side were out for 48. As all with any claim to historical knowledge are aware it was Hirst and Rhodes who got the last 15 of them for the last wicket. There are also two facts slightly less familiar, one that Jessop had been *dropped* from the preceding Test – selectors were only human, then as now! – and secondly when the two countries met at the Oval in this Fifth Test Australia had already retained the Ashes, just as England had done before the last Test on the same battle-ground in August, 1981. Yet the gates had to be closed. If a series really "takes off" The Ashes are almost a secondary consideration.

It was in 1903/4 that MCC took over, at the Australians' earnest request, the selection and management of English teams down under. This, too, is part of the legend of the game. "Plum" Warner had not previously played for England, nor was he first choice as captain. Yet after the Australians had won four series in a row he brought back The Ashes, which F. S. Jackson retained in England the following year, himself heading both batting and bowling averages.

I must skim lightly over the ground, pausing only at a few of the cross-roads: 1926, for instance, when the youthful Percy Chapman ended a depressing span of Australian supremacy by winning at the Oval. One sees clearly still the crowd spilling over and engulfing the England team at the end as they sped for shelter, the particular heroes, Hobbs and Sutcliffe, and Rhodes, recalled at 48 to play in his last Test, appearing in turn on the balcony to rounds of cheers.

Then came Bradman. As a youngster of 20 he played first in the 1928/9 series which Chapman won handsomely. This prodigious cricketer took part in the next seven series against England, being captain in the last four, and only once – in 1932/3 when Bodyline threatened to rupture Anglo-Australian relations – was he on the losing side. Nineteen 100s Don Bradman made against England – Hobbs's 12 for England comes next in the records – and as to his average of 89, only two men with anything approaching his number of appearances, Sutcliffe with 66 and Barrington with 63, come anywhere near him.

As after the First War so after the Second, English cricket, having been the harder hit, was the slower to recover. So it was 1953, Coronation Year, before Len Hutton brought home The Ashes after almost 20 years, and the Oval was once again the scene of rare national emotion.

England dominated now, thoroughly if briefly, winning in Australia, also under Hutton, in 1954/5 and, after his retirement, under Peter May in 1956. This was the year of Laker's staggering 19 wickets at Old Trafford and a for-ever record of 46 in the five-match series. This, by the way, was six years before the distinction between amateur and professional was abolished, and it is noteworthy that England's batting, apart from Cyril Washbrook, was amateur, the other five leaders in the Test averages being May himself, David Sheppard, now Bishop of Liverpool, Peter Richardson, Colin Cowdrey and Trevor Bailey.

The great Australian fast bowlers, Lindwall and Miller, were bowing out by the later '50s, but successors, not all with such beautiful actions, were soon in evidence, and the menace of throwing threatened relations in 1958/9 when Australia, with Richie Benaud captain, won with the utmost ease. Thanks to diplomacy at the highest level, wherein G. O. Allen and Sir Donald Bradman were the leading figures, the throwers disappeared as swiftly as they had come.

The '60s were perhaps the least fruitful time over the whole span of England-Australia matches, with 10 results only in 25 Tests, and either weather or wickets or a combination of both the common enemy. Three of the five series were halved, but Australia held on to the Ashes, albeit with difficulty, England's golden chance being at Old Trafford in 1961 when Benaud in an inspired spell snatched the game that Ted Dexter's brilliance had all but won. This was one of the classic Tests of my time, containing one of the most dramatic changes of fortune – until in this respect 1981 set new standards.

At long last the tide turned in 1970/1. Ray Illingworth was the victor, clinching the rubber 2-0 at Sydney in the last Test after Australia had broken a tradition of ancient standing by changing their captain (Ian Chappell for Lawrie). This was a series that brought a rebuke about conduct from the newly-formed Cricket Council, and it was followed by one of altogether superior vintage in 1972 when Illingworth retained the Ashes, although Australia squared the rubber 2-2 by winning a gripping last match at the Oval. In this summer Dennis Lillee and Greg Chappell emerged as great cricketers, and the former was due to be joined by another fast bowler of at least equal pace in Jeff Thomson.

Lillee and Thomson over the next two series submitted England to as severe a dose of speed as their predecessor had ever faced. No discredit attached to the losers of the rubbers of 1974/5 or of the following English summer when four Tests against Australia followed the wonderfully successful initiation of a Prudential World Cup. Tony Greig had succeeded Mike Denness in the England captaincy, and it was he who took his side on to Australia following a successful tour of India, in

March 1977, to play the Centenary Test in the great bowl of
Melbourne, on the same field that James Lillywhite's side had
trod precisely 100 years before.

The most sentimental occasion in cricket history, most
handsomely staged, produced cricket of a quality to match the
event, Lillee's bowling for Australia and Rodney Marsh's
hundred being complemented by Derek Randall's 174, the
innings of a life-time which seemed at one time as though it
might bring England to an incredible victory.

In the end, by a glorious fluke, England, having needed to
make 463 to win, lost by 45 runs – which was exactly the
margin of Australia's success back in March 1877. At this
moment all the omens for Test cricket were set fair. Public
appeal had never been greater, the atmosphere between the
sides was good, while a combination of the wonderful English
summers of 1975 and 1976, the success of the World Cup, and
the ever-increasing sums being brought into the game by
acceptable patronage, had brought it a welcome financial
viability. This, in turn, had already given more stability to the
first-class organizations of both countries and had been reflected
in higher rewards to the players.

As is now grim history, euphoria was short-lived. Less than
two months after Melbourne, with the Australians in England
for a full series, news broke of the wholesale defection of most
of the top Australians and a few Englishmen, headed by the
captain, plus numerous West Indians, Pakistanis and South
Africans. They had secretly contracted to play the following
winter in Australia for the proprietor of a commercial TV
company, Kerry Packer.

In an atmosphere of strained personal relations and much
off-the-field activity England, under Mike Brearley in that 1977
summer, regained the Ashes in the most decisive way by three
victories to none. Apart from Lillee, who had declared himself
unavailable under circumstances then known only to his com-
rades, this was a full-strength Australian side. When, however,
the next series came due in 1978/9 it was a necessarily make-
shift, unrepresentative Australian side that Brearley defeated by
the unprecedented margin (so far as England were concerned)
of 5-1.

When the Australian Cricket Board in the spring of 1979
came to an unexpectedly swift accommodation with World
Series Cricket, as the Packer organization styled itself, the Test
and County Cricket Board were almost implored to undertake

an extra – and extraordinary – tour of Australia in 1979/80, in company with the West Indies, to play a triangular series of one-day games (eleven no less) with three Tests and a few state fixtures. Under these conditions England declined to put The Ashes at stake. Australia won this rubber 3-0. England next staged at Lord's last year its own Centenary Test – which was won conclusively by the weather – which brings us, in abbreviated form at least, right up to date.

E. W. Swanton